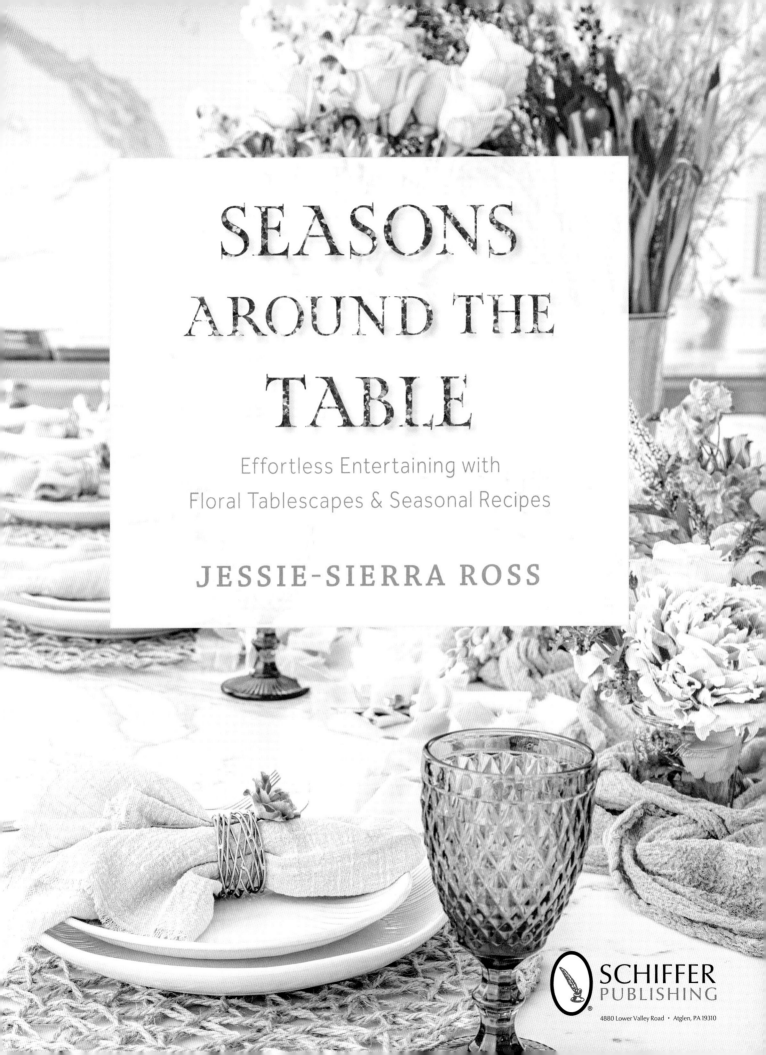

SEASONS AROUND THE TABLE

Effortless Entertaining with
Floral Tablescapes & Seasonal Recipes

JESSIE-SIERRA ROSS

SCHIFFER
PUBLISHING

4880 Lower Valley Road • Atglen, PA 19310

Copyright © 2024 by Jessie-Sierra Ross
Photography by Jonathan Ross

Library of Congress Control Number: 2024932137

Cover & Interior designed by Danielle D. Farmer
Cover photos by Jonathan Ross
Type set in Map Roman / Chaparral Pro / Effra

ISBN: 978-0-7643-6836-3
Printed in China

MIX
Paper | Supporting responsible forestry
FSC
www.fsc.org   FSC® C104723

Published by Schiffer Publishing, Ltd.
4880 Lower Valley Road
Atglen, PA 19310
Phone: (610) 593-1777; Fax: (610) 593-2002
Email: Info@schifferbooks.com
Web: www.schifferbooks.com

For our complete selection of fine books on this and related subjects, please visit our website at www.schifferbooks.com. You may also write for a free catalog.

Schiffer Publishing's titles are available at special discounts for bulk purchases for sales promotions or premiums. Special editions, including personalized covers, corporate imprints, and excerpts, can be created in large quantities for special needs. For more information, contact the publisher.

We are always looking for people to write books on new and related subjects. If you have an idea for a book, please contact us at proposals@schifferbooks.com.

To Mum, Nana Barbara,
and Baba Dina;
I will always save a
seat at the table for you.

CONTENTS

Introduction | 9

 Vegetarian (V)    Gluten-Free (GF)   Vegan | *Also see "Vegan and Gluten-Free Changes for Selected Recipes" on page 235.*

Spring

Summer

Autumn

Winter

INTRODUCTION

One of my earliest memories is of baking cookies at my mother's side. I was about six years old, all gangly limbs and braided hair, watching my mother use an old hand mixer to cream together butter and sugar. I was fascinated by the whirling beaters and stared spellbound at the incredible transformation of basic ingredients into a beautiful cookie batter.

My little hands got the job of dumping gobs of chocolate chips into the bowl. Being a bit impish, I of course snuck a few for myself. Food was the most basic form of love in my house. Just like the chocolate chips that I stealthily scarfed down, the act of cooking was sweet and, for me, addictive!

As I grew up, so did my love of all things culinary. Sunday afternoons were filled with black-and-white reruns of Julia Child on public broadcasting, and I don't think I ever missed an episode of Martha Stewart's early work. They were as captivating to me as any fairy tale; an escape into a world that seemed so much bigger and grander than my parents' very tiny house in the city.

When my career as a young ballet dancer took off, food for me changed to take on more of a double edge: both loved and hated, food became fuel. The lifestyle of a professional ballerina is not for the faint of heart, and it was hard to keep from indulging in the decadent treats that make the rounds at performance galas and benefactor cocktail parties. Even with that sort of physical denial, my mental appreciation for the artistry of food, and my sense of dramatic storytelling from the theater, continued to build. I wanted to learn more. More about cooking. More about technique. More about plating. More about serving with elegance. I started thinking about food as a performance, as much as it was a sensory experience.

Just as with dance, presenting food involves a touch of the spectacular, and the intertwining of floral elements with food had an interesting starting-off point for me. I grew up with flowers—my grandmother had a genuine green thumb, and memories of her are always mixed with images of roses the size of dessert plates—but the real connection came to me when I was thinking about centerpieces for my wedding. At the time, we didn't have the budget for table decorations, so I ordered some inexpensive rectangular plates and loose sheaves of flowers, and bought fruit from the grocer. I plated everything right at the venue, wearing half a wedding dress and with my hair in pins. It was a hit—and the centerpiece fruit was a great snack before the food started coming out of the kitchens!

When I left my career as a professional ballet dancer, I began diving into cooking and home entertaining in earnest. I suddenly found myself with large parcels of time, and even more of curiosity. Having moved from the roaring city to the relative countryside of Western Massachusetts, I was at an epicenter of farm-fresh ingredients. I realized very quickly the difference that from-scratch cooking—with respectful treatment of high-quality ingredients—made, and it was the way I wanted to live. With my new access to wide-open spaces, I dove into the world of botanicals and edible homegrown flowers. And most importantly, I started to incorporate them into my formal and informal food and entertaining concepts.

Now, how would I share that idea?

When I first started throwing parties and dinners, I didn't know where to begin! Menu planning? Table decor? What about wines or cocktails? Should I call the florist for a centerpiece or run to the grocery store for a quick bouquet?

I gradually noticed that there was a sort of basic formula to creating these events. As the years went by, I realized that with just a smidge more planning, I could host gatherings that would stay in the memories of my guests! I began by creating cohesive menus that were sure to have a big impact at the table but not leave me sweating in the kitchen. After all, if a party is as enjoyable for you as your guests, you're going to want to do more of them! And the table itself, with floral touches and small details, became part of the story the food was telling.

I want you to shake off the notion that home entertaining is a thing of the past, that it's something reserved for that generation of grandmothers who attended antiquated etiquette classes and innately knew the difference between a dessert and salad fork. Home entertaining can be as intricate or as beautifully simple as you choose it to be. In my home, modern hosting draws from beautiful and elegant aspects of the past and streamlines the process for those of us still seeking to connect over a supper party, or to bring the thrill of a festive holiday dinner to our friends and family.

Let's set the table together and whip up meals that will leave your guests delighted and allow you to keep your focus where it belongs—on great times and superb company!

How This Book Works

Having a basic structure is one of the easiest ways to start. I share that with you here, together with options to use from my favorite seasonal recipes and menus, color schemes, flower tricks, and tips for hosting an event to remember. However, these are just blueprints! You are in control of the how, the why, and the reason.

For each season, I've written several unique themed menus. I've included everything from original cocktails and mains to fresh sides and desserts. Along with being taste sensations, they're often floral inspired. Additionally, I've shared my personal favorite tablescapes and themed color schemes, as well seasonally inspired floral arrangements. In my world, flowers are just as much a style statement as the food. Whether you're new to flowers and arranging them, or already an enthusiast, this book is designed to help guide your perspective and help you take your table to the next level. Whether from your garden or the grocery florist, your events can be spectacular and beautiful if you design them with some principal elements in mind.

You will also find some helpful guides for essential ingredients, my favorite floral-arranging tools, kitchen must-haves, basic color theory, and edible flowers. This book is meant to be your own personal party planner, menu coordinator, cooking school, and florist advisor! Pick and choose what you like and weave the ideas into your own designs!

My hope is that you can turn to any chapter in this book and find everything you need to host the party of your dreams! It empowers you to not only get to work in the kitchen, and set your table with aplomb, but to also become known in your circle as the "person who hosts"!

Eating with the seasons is a passion of mine, but if you live in a place with cold winters, it can be a long wait to bring fresh produce to the menu. When I think it is helpful to the overarching theme of the menu, I will feature fruits and vegetables that are available year-round in grocery stores. I've also made sure that we are keeping up with the times by including many recipes that are catered to those with special dietary restrictions or those who abstain from grains, animal proteins, or animal products by preference. The modern host needs to be flexible without sacrificing taste or quality, so I've made sure these recipes are full of flavor and treated as artfully as any other recipe in the book. Vegetarian, vegan, and gluten-free recipes are marked.

There are others that can be relatively easily substituted to fit some of these life options, which you will find in an index on page 235. Cocktails and beverages are usually vegetarian, vegan, and gluten-free, so their recipes are not coded. Check them to determine your substitution preferences.

Finally, I want to add a note about mindset. I think it is easy to fall into the idea that you have to bake/cook/make everything yourself. If you want to pick up a precooked dish and mix it in with recipes here, or have a centerpiece made and mix it with other elements you have at home, that's absolutely what you should do! Home entertaining isn't about being perfect, and it isn't about doing everything. It's about having the best time possible with family and friends. Make that your priority, and for everything you want to do yourself, this book is here to help!

My wish is for every budding host to take the leap and dive fully into the world of home entertaining and inspired cooking. With just a little guidance, and a smidge of confidence from this reformed ballerina, you can absolutely throw all the dinner parties and gatherings that you've ever imagined for your friends, family, and, of course, yourself to enjoy!

About Measurements

Living in America, I tend to think in cups and ounces for cooking. This is not the case for most parts of the world, so I have provided weight-based metric conversions. In examining databases to aid in this process, I was not always satisfied with the results I was getting, which could be off by 10%–40% from my personal measurements. Long story short, I measured and weighed every ingredient out to make sure you are using the same amounts that I am using when cooking or baking. For liquids: when I felt it was contributing to the dish (as in baking) I use more precise measurements, for example 1 cup of water = 238 ml. When I deemed that level of precision to not be needed, for example in pouring 1 ounce for a cocktail, or 10 cups for boiling water, I have rounded the numbers so that one liquid cup would equal 250 ml, which is a common equivalency.

Creating Tablescapes

The key to creating beautiful tablescapes is to start by asking the right questions. I display several holiday and event tablescape designs in this book, to help get you going. Your own spin on these examples is what will really speak to your guests! A table setting can be as formal or as informal as you wish. It can be rich with details, like Grandma's heirloom china plates or your finest crystal, but it can also be cool and casual, with bright touches that reflect your own personal style.

I tend to envisage my tablescape designs from a few different viewpoints. Before I begin pulling out any dishes or silverware, I ask myself a few easy questions to help focus my thinking. I want to identify the following:

IS THERE A THEME OR SPECIFIC HOLIDAY I'M DESIGNING FOR?

If there is a theme that you're decorating for, then you want to make sure that you identify the crucial elements, such as color palettes or traditional decorations, that will work within your scene. This provides a flexible framework to build outward from. Is there a specific plate, decorative piece, or functional art piece that is meaningful for your theme? Put it down on the table! This is the time to consider how to incorporate it.

SEASONALITY: WHAT FLOWERS ARE AVAILABLE?

Seasonality is just as important for flowers as it is for our other recipe ingredients. For example, sourcing those gorgeous spring pink peonies isn't going to be easy if you're setting up a Christmas table in December! Identifying what flower varieties are available, and when, is very helpful before you hit the flower market!

WHAT IS THE TOTAL NUMBER OF GUESTS EXPECTED?

The expected number of guests is also crucial to planning and executing your tablescapes. A small cozy dinner party for four will need fewer decorative elements or settings. A Thanksgiving dinner for sixteen will need as much table space as you can muster. Between the place settings, the flowers, and whether you're choosing an informal versus formal setting, this type of large-scale tablescape will need room to create a lush scene for your guests to enjoy.

The Three Rules of Tablescapes

There is a basic formula to setting up the perfect table, and it is a flexible set of guidelines that I follow each and every time I'm entertaining. I refined these elements over the years to focus on a low-stress setup, while still delivering the greatest impact.

1. INFORMAL VS. FORMAL

Before you start polishing the silver, you want to decide whether your table settings will be informal or formal. There are several degrees of formality, but I tend to stick to informal table settings for brunches, showers, and luncheons, while reserving formal table settings for big holiday dinners and dinner parties. There are only a few tweaks between the two styles, but they do make a world of difference to the feeling at the table.

Informal

An informal table is just as it sounds: a little more relaxed; a tad more casual. They're excellent for parties where there will be a smaller number of courses. It's more elevated than a "family style" plate of eggs in the middle of the table for breakfast, but not intricate like a Buckingham Palace dinner!

My *informal* table style consists of a place mat or charger at each seat, followed by a dinner plate, a salad plate, and an optional soup bowl. For silverware, the basic cutlery of knife, fork, and spoon is all you need. Although I tend to set it up with the knife and soup spoon on the right of the plates, and a dinner fork on the left, they can all be bundled together or wrapped in a napkin or placed on one side. When I'm trying to up the game a little bit, I will include a smaller salad fork on the outer left, because it adds a nice balance and also feels a bit fancy. I tend to place napkins either under the forks or on top of the salad plate. Glassware is minimal; a water glass on the top right, and optionally a wineglass to the right of that.

Formal

A true *formal* table has many place-setting elements: several types of silverware and glasses, as well as bread plates and butter knives. This reflects the fact that a formal dinner typically has three or more courses served, each with its own utensil! My personal formal style tends toward the Western format but strays from the traditional—that's the beauty of hosting your own parties!

I like to start with a place mat or decorative charger, then add both a dinner plate and a salad plate on top. Optionally, you can add a soup bowl, depending on your menu. In regard to the silverware, on the left-hand side of the plate we have a small salad fork and a dinner fork. On the right-hand side, we have a dinner knife and a soup spoon. I also like to include a dessert spoon at the very top of the setting, just opposite the dinner plate.

Glassware will include a water glass and a red-wine glass in the same positions as the informal setting, with an added white-wine glass on the lower right. Napkins may be placed underneath the forks, on top of the salad plates, or folded in the red-wine glasses. A bread plate and butter knife may be placed on the upper left corner, but for modern hosting, I've seen this tradition fall away.

From reading this description, it may seem that many of the table elements are the same as the *informal* style above. Of course, all tables have plates and cutlery and glassware. The distinction for me is in the *types* of elements I use. I do always encourage people to bring out their best china and set their heirloom silverware in this type of event. These pieces are meant to be used and enjoyed! Instead of gathering dust in a box, these beautiful items can be the stars of the table! That crystal decorative piece you received for a wedding present, or a special vase that you have on display—this is the time to show them off, in a prominent spot on your table!

Still, don't worry if you don't have all of these pieces for a formal setting; use what you have! Your dishware doesn't have to match, your red-wine glasses can be used for white, and your formal silverware may still be in storage. These are just suggestions!

2. LIGHT, COLOR, TEXTURE

Now that the formality level of your party has been squared away, we can talk light, color, and texture. These three little words make all the difference to your tablescape. Incorporating small elements from each of these categories can create a huge impact.

Light

Lighting truly does set the mood for any party, and I believe it makes a huge difference on your table! Small glass votives spaced along the table runner, paired with long tapers in crystal candlesticks, add a touch of warm light and really change the feel of your event. There is something elemental and satisfying about the flicker of candlelight at a dinner table, and I am a big proponent of it.

Experiment by mixing and matching your styles of candlesticks. Elegant silver or crystal candlesticks lend a touch of class for a formal table, while chunky wooden pillars bring a homey feeling to an informal event. Small ornamental candleholders of different colors will have a dazzling effect when chosen to highlight the

overall theme of the event, and they take up less space than their bigger counterparts. I also like to play with a variety of different types of candles. I love richly colored tapers, but pure beeswax candles and chunky pillars are lovely when paired with the right base.

Lighting is an area where you can really individualize your table and create a unique mood for your guests. It's not just candlelight that can set the scene. Imagine a lush garden, with multiple ornate lit lanterns guiding your guests along a gravel path. Under a pergola strung with softly glowing string lights, tables overflow with beautiful flowers in small jars, and trays of cocktails. It's a pretty picture, right?

Color

Color can help tell a story or set a seasonal "feel" to your table. Deciding on how you will approach the colors on your table ahead of time simplifies your flower choices, as well as your table-setting plans. Although there are six principal color theory palettes, I like to pick one of the "big three" when it comes to tablescapes:

A **complementary** palette (pick two colors that are on opposite sides of the color wheel), a monochromatic/achromatic palette (multiple tones and shades of the same single color, or shade of white), or an analogous palette (where you pick three colors that sit right beside each other on the color wheel).

Great examples of complementary color choices are red and green for Christmas. They are opposites on the color wheel and just pop when on the table! Paired with white, silver, and gold elements, this gives you a colorful, festive scene!

Monochromatic/achromatic colors are especially easy to put together and always look very elegant. You'll take one color in different tones and shades, or start with white (achromatic) and slowly shade it to black or a single color to create a striking floral piece or table. Setting a table with different shades of white and creams is a wonderful example of elegant monochromatic/achromatic color use.

Analogous colors are very pleasing to the eye. Any three colors that sit in order on the color wheel create a harmonious color story. The centerpiece for the "baby shower" event in this book follows this pattern, with pink, violet, and purple flowers. These analogous colors form a very pulled-together look for the table.

The simplest way to incorporate color to your table is via your flowers, linens, and small pieces of decor that you add to the table. I usually keep my dishware fairly neutral but add big, bold pops of color elsewhere throughout the tablescape.

Texture

Texture is often the aspect that gets forgotten about when planning a table, but you will be amazed at the difference it makes in the overall impression of the scene. Texture can be provided from woven place mats, rough-spun napkins, or embroidered linens, or even in the more intricate details of an objet d'art that you place beside each table setting. These can be found in the home goods sections of many stores, at almost any price point, but whenever I can, I try to use items that are either handcrafted or found in nature. One of my favorite ways to bring texture to a table is to incorporate organic shapes in the form of fruits, gourds, natural grasses, and even pine cones.

Flower arrangements automatically add textures to the tablescape you're creating. The dramatic effect can be furthered with dried seed pods, branches, grasses, and vines to incorporate more of the natural world into our homes. Working different textures into your tablescapes provides loads of unexpected and enchanting details and can bring a lot of whimsy to your designs.

3. THE RULE OF THREE

When it comes to arranging your pieces on the table, the best advice I have is to follow the "Rule of Three." This refers to our natural inclination to prefer objects grouped into odd numbers. Interior designers and artists use this trick all the time—and so can you! Whether it's used in home decorating or in tablescapes, most people innately find odd numbers of objects to be more visually appealing than even ones. Three seems to be the most effective, but any odd number works!

Arranging your candlesticks in groups of three is an easy way to create a fresh point of visual interest. Adding small jars filled with vibrantly colored flowers, in groupings of three or five, along the length of the table, is a super-simple way of playing with our innate love of odd numbers in decorating!

Kitchen Tools

I would be fibbing if I didn't admit that I get excited about kitchen gadgets! I thumb through the glossy pages for the latest pots, knives, and gizmos every time the newest catalog comes in the mail. But outside of staring at the latest and greatest, there are a variety of tools (other than good pots and pans) that I consider *essential* to whip up the best meals.

I'm going to share my favorite kitchen tools that I use all the time, and that will make your life so much easier!

A HEAVY-DUTY STAND MIXER. I'm not saying that your trusty handheld mixer can't do the job, but a professional-style stand mixer is *such* a pleasure to work with in the kitchen! From making a bread dough to beating egg whites, a stand mixer gives you the power, and the attachments, that you need to create a variety of sauces, batters, and doughs.

LARGE, NONSTICK BAKING SHEETS. I know that it sounds very basic, but having several high-quality nonstick baking sheets can make or break your baking. I prefer nonstick baking sheets with a rim. They are a utilitarian choice for almost everything, whether you are baking cookies, toasting nuts, or roasting vegetables.

A LARGE FOOD PROCESSOR. One of the most popular housewarming/wedding gifts out there, a food processor is a workhorse in the kitchen. Whether you want to slice, blend a chimichurri, or create a quick pie dough, my food processor is a time-saving joy.

A 9-INCH (23 CM) NONSTICK SPRINGFORM PAN. The specialized baking pan is perfect for whipping up a cheesecake or a batch of cinnamon rolls. Its unique ability to remove the sides of the pan, without disrupting the inner contents, makes this a beautiful choice for specialty pastries.

A LARGE CAST-IRON SKILLET. Cast iron is wonderful for searing proteins, acting as a water jacket for baking, or simply frying up a bunch of eggs for breakfast! Its weight and molecular makeup hold and spread the heat from your cooking element in a way that few other materials can.

AT LEAST ONE HIGH-QUALITY 7-INCH SANTOKU-STYLE KNIFE. One of the very first tools that I invested in as a new cook was a high-quality Japanese Santoku. It's versatile, lightweight, and perfectly balanced. I know that if you ask a professional chef, they will quickly recommend a chef's knife rather than a Santoku, but if you're not spending eight hours a day in the kitchen, rocking the knife back and forth, to chop vegetables, you will probably love the Santoku style more. The shape is better to chop with, it's lighter in weight, and it is much easier to control, because of the shorter overall length. I gave my chef's knife away when I got the Santoku.

A KNIFE SHARPENER. Contrary to what most people think, sharp knives are much safer to use than dull knives, because there is less chance of the blade slipping off the food and landing on your fingers!

A MANDOLINE. This is a nifty tool in the kitchen, especially if you are looking to create precisely cut thin slices of food. Extremely sharp, but easy to use, a mandoline slicer lets you cut gorgeous and consistent potato rounds or apple slices so quickly that you will barely believe it. Because it is so sharp, always use the guard when using to protect your fingers.

LARGE WOODEN CUTTING BOARDS. Although a little bit trickier to clean than their plastic counterparts, heavyweight wooden cutting boards are my preferred cutting surface. They are also excellent to use while assembling pastry or rolling out doughs.

STAINLESS-STEEL COCKTAIL SHAKERS. I keep several two-piece "Boston" shakers in my bar cabinets. Lightweight, yet sturdy, these stainless-steel cocktail shakers are versatile and easy to clean.

A HAWTHORNE STRAINER. There are many ways to strain a cocktail into a glass, but I find the Hawthorne strainer to be simple to use and foolproof (it's the one you hold on the top of a glass or shaker, with a coiled wire around the edge to hold the ice back as you pour).

A MULTIPURPOSE MEASURING SHOT GLASS OR JIGGER. This is a handy little cocktail tool that lets you precisely measure out your liquids. I prefer the marked glass versions to the traditional metal ones, since they are easier to read.

A DIGITAL SCALE. I've only recently turned to this tool, but now I can't live without it! Digital scales are excellent for weighting out precise amounts of dry goods or liquids, so that you get the right results each time you make a recipe. I prefer the water-resistant stainless-steel versions, and there are many affordable options on the market.

A DIGITAL MEAT THERMOMETER. This is an incredible must-have tool for meats and larger poultry such as turkey—I never want to go back to oven roasting without it! Get something with a digital display, but not one that you have to open the oven to use, or to read—you lose a lot of heat from your oven every time you open it, and can significantly change the cooking time! My newest thermometer is a wireless one and has a Bluetooth connection to my phone that provides continuous temperature monitoring, but older wired models (with thin wires that reach out of the oven to an external display), or the ones that plug into a port in the oven itself, still work beautifully.

Ingredient Essentials for Everyday Entertaining

There is an expectation that every accomplished host has an overflowing pantry full of prepared gourmet foods and a refrigerator bursting with a plethora of fresh ingredients to throw the best dinner party or casual get-together . . . that's simply not the case! You can create an outstanding cocktail night, or even a full brunch, with just a few common ingredients on hand. I like to keep this list stocked in my kitchen, so I'm ready at a moment's notice to pull together tasty finger foods or a delicious cocktail!

PANTRY AND COUNTER

CRACKERS. Whether stoneground wheat, crispy rice, or sea salt almond meal, shelf-stable crackers are the way to go for easy entertaining. Pair them with a white bean dip and fresh veggies or use them to add crunch to a charcuterie board. Crackers create the perfect base for a variety of party foods.

PICKLED VEGETABLES. It may sound old school, but having a variety of pickled veggies in your pantry can add zip to salads or an acidic zing to any cheese board. I love these vinegary fermented foods so much that I have a whole shelf devoted to them! Choices like black or green olives add a great fattiness to many dishes. Small French cornichons, or spicy dill pickles, create contrast. Even pickled beets or green beans can be used to add balance to a plate!

FRESH CITRUS. You'll often hear me repeat one of my favorite mottos when I'm filming a cocktail TV segment: Fresh is best. Seriously, for fruit juices there isn't any comparison. I like to keep a small basket of fresh lemons, limes, and oranges on my kitchen counter at all times. The fresh juices are sweet and sour and pop on the tongue in a way that presqueezed can't match. You can easily use them in baking, for creating spectacular desserts, in cocktails or cocktail syrups, and even in gourmet sauces. Fresh citrus on hand is a must, in my book.

DRIED FRUITS. Yes, I just said "fresh is best" in the paragraph above, but it's not the only side of the story! Dried fruits are a great way to add that punch of vine-ripened sweet flavor to any meal, even in the winter! I like to keep dried apricots, cherries, prunes, and cranberries in my pantry to add to salads, desserts, and baked goods. You can even make delicious infused simple syrups with a handful of dried fruits!

BAKING INGREDIENTS. Flour, sugar, baking soda, and baking powder. When in doubt, you can always bake up an easy fruit crumble for dessert, or a marvelous stack of crepes for breakfast with just these basic ingredients.

DRIED SPICES. We are talking about more than just the dynamic duo of salt and black pepper! Smoked paprika, allspice berries, cinnamon, green cardamom, dried lavender, pungent ginger, dried chili, fresh nutmeg, and ground cloves. Spice brings life to a dish and lets you play with lots of flavors! Remember to refresh your spice rack every six months, if possible.

THE REFRIGERATOR AND FREEZER

BUTTER. Whether salted or sweet cream, butter is essential for so many sauces, pastries, and spreads. It's also so easy to freeze!

HIGH-QUALITY CHEESES. Brie, Parmigiano Reggiano, and good cheddars, oh my! Cheese has my heart, and it's the perfect versatile ingredient to keep on hand for easy home entertaining. Stunning on its own, or paired with crackers and a fruit spread, cheese can be transformed into beautifully creamy sauces and incorporated into pastries. Keep a selection of sheep and cow's milk cheeses of soft, firm, and hard varieties in the fridge. Throw them together on a platter with some already cooked smoked sausage, or a bit of prosciutto, and you have an easy and yummy charcuterie board for your guests.

PUFF PASTRY. You might not think this premade freezer-case product would find its way into my kitchen, but it's incredibly versatile! You can make a quick quiche in moments, using puff pastry for the crust, or whip up individual tarts with sweet pears and Manchego cheese, all with the same package! Puff pastry is easy to use, and even easier to store.

HEAVY CREAM. Used to thicken sauces or to make a fluffy whipped cream for a cake, heavy cream is a versatile ingredient and an essential in my refrigerator. I use it for sauces and drinks, and it's an easy way to add a beautiful mouth feel to so many recipes.

EGGS. Eggs can be part of a recipe, or the main event. From a quick brunch quiche to that floaty foam that tops a traditional gin sour cocktail, eggs are an important part of cooking, baking, and mixology. Finding an egg replacement is also pretty easy; aquafaba (chickpea water) for cocktails is a wonderful vegan alterative for drinks. For baking, ground flaxseed mixed with a bit of water works well as an egg replacement.

SEASONAL FRUIT. Enjoy produce in season. It's more likely to be local, and when ingredients don't have to travel far, it can be picked when it's more ripe, and much more delicious. Where I live, this means berries in late spring, stone fruits in summer, apples and pears in the fall, and plenty of citrus in the winter. Fresh seasonal fruits add color and flavor to any recipe.

FRESH HERBS. I like to grow my own fresh herbs during the summer, but store-packaged fresh herbs work just as well. Just like citrus, fresh herbs have a distinct flavor difference that can completely change a dish compared to their dried counterparts. I like to buy at least one type of basil, thyme, rosemary, and cilantro as my basic stock, and during the summers I grow Thai basil, lemon thyme, chives, parsley, and dill. Tossing hand-torn herb leaves into a salad gives you instant flavor and aroma! Create an infused simple syrup with fresh rosemary or thyme to add a green herbaceous note to a batch cocktail. Blend a handful of fresh basil into a salad dressing, and you will get plenty of oohs and ahhhs at the table! Herbs are an easy way to elevate the most basic recipe.

Flower Ingredients

There's no doubt about it: one of the best ways to bring the beauty of nature to your cooking is to garnish with fresh flowers and herbs! With their beautiful colors, scents, and textures, fresh blooms can elevate any dish! However, it's vital to know what varieties are safe to eat, and also to distinguish that from the terms "food-safe" and "edible flowers."

Although these two terms seem interchangeable, in the food world they have quite different meanings!

EDIBLE FLOWERS, as the term implies, are completely safe for consumption. This means that the flower itself is safe to eat, presuming it has not been treated with any pesticides, added chemicals, or preservatives, as described below. (Edible does not always mean delicious, but they are as safe to eat as any common salad item!)

FOOD-SAFE FLOWERS, on the other hand, should follow the same growing rules, but these are varieties of flowers that shouldn't generally be eaten. These are good choices to act as decorations or added flourish, but they should be removed before enjoying your cocktail or dish. They won't cause you serious harm if you do end up eating them, but it's best not to ingest them.

Not only does any plant you might use need to be nonpoisonous and nonharmful to a person to begin with, but it must also be grown and cared for in a safe way for consumption. For flowers to be considered edible, they need to be grown without the use of pesticides or added chemicals, and they need to be picked, packaged, and shipped in a responsible fashion. This understandably limits where we can purchase those beautiful edible blooms for your next recipe.

Clearly, flowers you would consider putting in your food or drink must be grown from a trusted source. Traditional commercial florist bouquets, flowering plants from nurseries, and grocery store flowers are not considered edible or food-safe, since the flowers are grown in fields with chemical pesticides and fertilizers. Additionally, the flowers are often sprayed with chemical preservatives before shipping to your local vendor, to ensure freshness and color. It may work for a centerpiece, but it's definitely not something that we want to eat at the dinner table!

Instead, here are some ways to find edible flowers in your area.

Commercially Produced Edible Flowers

Sometimes found packaged in the fresh-herb section of your local grocery store or organic market, there are a number of companies that specifically grow and ship edible flowers for use. This is a very convenient option for the home cook, and because these farmers are held to strict growing practices, the flowers are certified as edible.

Online Small-Scale Commercial Flower Farms

Another alternative is to hop online and find smaller-scale commercial flower farms that offer edible flowers for sale. I often turn to this resource, since they have more variety, and I like to support small businesses. Although they're slightly pricier, I have found smaller flower farms to produce higher-quality blooms in general.

Be sure to check their websites for language that states that they are pesticide and chemical free, as well as following proper environmentally sound practices for growing, harvesting, packaging, and shipping. If they aren't up-front with this information, move on to the next producer.

Local Certified-Organic Flower Farms and Farmers' Markets

A lovely perk of the "farm-to-table" lifestyle is the wide variety of floral options that can be found at farmers' markets and local certified-organic flower farms. Farmers' markets are a wonderful place to shop for fresh produce, baked goods, and seasonal flowers! Be sure to have a conversation with the vendor before purchasing any flowers, to ensure that they are grown without undesirable chemicals or pesticides. (As always, check to make sure that the types of blossoms themselves are not poisonous for consumption!)

The same rules apply to buying from any local flower farm. Scan their websites or have a direct conversation with the farmer, to learn more about their growing and harvesting practices.

Here are my favorite edible and food-safe flowers to use on my own table.

EDIBLE FLOWERS

Alyssum	Cilantro blossoms	Orchid
Amaranth blossoms	Chrysanthemum	Pansies
Arugula blossoms	Cosmos (*sulphureus* species only)	Primrose
Aster	Daisies	Rose
Bachelor's button (cornflower)	Dahlia	Rose-scented geraniums
Basil blossoms	Dianthus	Snapdragons
Bee balm	Dill blossoms	Sunflowers
Borage	Elderflower blossoms	Thai mint blossoms
Butterfly blue pea blossoms	Fennel blossoms	Thyme blossoms
Buzz button	Hibiscus blossoms	Viola
Calendula blossoms	Hollyhocks	Violets
Carnation	Lavender blossoms	Zinnias
Chamomile blossoms	Marigolds	
Chive blossoms	Nasturtium blossoms	

FOOD-SAFE FLOWERS
(These are for garnish or decoration only due to taste)

Allium	Camellia	Gerbera
Bellis daisy	Dandelion blossoms	Lilac
Bergamot	Echinacea blossoms	Peony
Busy lizzie (impatiens)	Freesia	Wax flower

Easy Flowers and Herbs to Grow at Home

Fresh, edible flowers are something that brings joy to my everyday living. If you enjoy gardening as much as I do, growing your own edible flowers might be your best solution for sourcing beautiful blooms! Whether you have a garden bed ready to use, or you're a fan of container gardening, everyone can grow these varieties of edible flowers and herbs. As a bonus, growing your own flowers can help support your local honeybee and pollinator population!

EASILY HOMEGROWN VARIETIES
(in temperate climates)

I live in US Zone 6a, but you can find the right list for your own location via a quick search on the web. Type in your location and "what growing zone," and you'll get some results quickly.

Alyssum	Cosmos	Pansies
Bachelors button (cornflower)	Dahlia	Pineapple sage
Basil	Daylily	Rose
Bee balm	Dianthus	Rose-scented geranium
Borage	Dill	Snapdragons
Calendula	Fennel	Sunflowers
Carnation	Lavender	Thyme
Chamomile	Honeysuckle	Violets
Chives	Marigold	Zinnias
Cilantro flower	Mint	Zucchini blossoms
Clover	Nasturtium	

Floral-Arranging Tools

Floral arranging is an art of its own! There are many options for mixing colors, textures, shapes, and variety in order to incorporate seasonality and theme. You might be asking yourself at this point, what exactly do I need to get started? With just a few simple tools and supplies, you will be on your way to creating your own spectacular floral creations!

VASES AND VESSELS

Almost any water-holding vessel can act as a container for your next bouquet! Whether it's a broad-based milk glass bowl, or a beautiful antique crystal vase, the vessel that holds your flowers will have an impact on the shape and feel of the arrangement. I have a number of different types of vases, vessels, and glasses to bring different moods to my tablescapes.

You can find many varieties at different home goods shops and online, but don't forget your local thrift stores. There are hidden gems just waiting to be picked up for your next floral composition. Even better? They're extremely affordable!

Some staples for your home should include

8-OUNCE GLASS JAM JARS. These are wonderful for making low and tidy arrangements with a lot of playfulness.

8- AND 12-INCH GLASS CYLINDER VASES. A classic for a reason, cylinder vases are great for more-elegant arrangements with some draping elements.

LARGE COMPOTE VASES OR BOWLS (a compote bowl is essentially a bowl on a pedestal). These can be made of distressed metal, stone, ceramic, or glass. This type of vase is both broad in shape and also elevated from the tabletop, making it perfect for statement arrangements.

VINTAGE CERAMIC OR CRYSTAL VASES AND BOWLS. There's nothing like an antique vase to set the tone of elegance on your table! You can find these pieces online or in vintage stores.

NOVELTY VASES. I have several of these in my pantry. They can help illustrate a specific theme or mood you want to bring to your table. Cement Roman busts, square wooden containers with liners, wicker baskets with plastic inserts, and even galvanized steel buckets are great statement pieces.

FLORAL FROGS, PILLOWS, AND TAPE

Once you've chosen your vessel, it's time to think about how we will stabilize our flowers within the vase. There are a couple of options, and here are a few of my favorites!

FLORAL FROGS. Although it looks more like a hedgehog than a frog, this tool is an age-old method of securing your flower arrangements. A flower frog, sometimes called a pin frog, is an easy, environmentally safe tool to give your flowers a secure foundation. They can be made from a variety of materials, including ceramic, metal, or plastic, but you want to look for a flower frog that is fairly heavy and has long pins arranged close together. Some flower frogs eliminate the need for pins altogether and feature a disc with several tightly packed holes instead. Both versions are very handy. Simply place at the bottom of your vase or vessel, fill with your treated water (see below), and then start arranging.

FLORAL PILLOWS. Floral pillows are an interesting reusable floral tool for securing arrangements. Made of sturdy plastic, these two-sided "pillows" feature a geometric grid pattern to place your flowers inside. They come in a variety of shapes and sizes, making it easy to use for any type of vase or vessel.

FLORAL TAPE AND SCOTCH TAPE. Having a few rolls of tape on hand is well worth it! Floral tape is a strong, waterproof tape that helps secure your flowers when creating more-structural shapes like wreaths or garlands. I also like to have a roll of scotch tape on hand to create bespoke grids on my vases. By making a grid of tape over the mouth of the vase or vessel, you have a simple way to secure your floral arrangement.

Note: You've probably noticed that I didn't mention floral foam, and this is due to problems with biodegradation. Many florists and floral professionals are moving away from the green, spongy foam, preferring other methods of securing their flowers. If you do feel most comfortable with floral foam, I highly recommend looking for a biodegradable version.

CLIPS, SNIPS, AND FLOWER FOOD

If you're diving into the world of floral arranging, you're going to be doing a lot of trimming and cutting to get your flowers into tip-top shape. From trimming away excess foliage to cutting your flower stems to height, having a sharp set of pruners or clippers is a necessity.

Cut-flower food will also be needed to prolong the life of your arrangement, and to make sure the colors stay vibrant. Flower food not only feeds your flowers while in the vase but also slows bacterial growth in the water they sit in. You can buy it in bulk or make your own. An easy homemade recipe is to combine 2 tablespoons (30 ml) of lemon juice, 1 tablespoon (13 g) of sugar, and 2–3 drops of household bleach to a quart (1 L) of lukewarm water.

Trim your spent flowers and foliage and change the water every two to three days to extend your bouquet's shelf life.

Spring

This is the season of joyous renewal, both in the garden and at the table! The spring holidays are the perfect way to reconnect with loved ones after a long winter's hibernation. New green shoots push through the dark soil, and a patchwork of pink and purple blooms helps us celebrate the return of warmer days!

It is also the season for tender new vegetables and fresh green herbs. Green peas, bright citrus, early berries with fresh sweet cream, and roasted meats flavored with just-picked garlic and thyme . . . Our tables are laden not only with tastes of spring, but also with bountiful bundles of delicate ranunculus, tulips, and lilacs. Warm breezes drift through the soft flower petals as the world wakes to a new season!

SPRING MENUS

SPRING HOLIDAY LUNCH

LEMON GIN FLORA

A light and floral traditional gin sour. Sweet and citrusy, this bright-yellow cocktail is like a sunny day in a glass!

CREAMY BASIL DIP WITH FRESH VEGETABLES

A fresh appetizer platter that welcomes the season by pairing tasty vegetables with a creamy, herbaceous, garlic-kissed dip. The dip can be made up to two days before, if needed.

CITRUS AND ROASTED BEET SALAD WITH HONEYED VINAIGRETTE

Sweet citrus and earthy cinnamon-spiced roasted beets is a match made in heaven! Garnished with fresh basil leaves and topped with a light honey-champagne vinegar dressing. The dressing can be made up to three days before, and the beets can be roasted up to two days before.

SOUS VIDE LEG OF LAMB WITH ROSEMARY AND MINT

A stunning main course that will leave your guests impressed! We'll season a lamb leg with fresh herbs and garlic, then pop it into the sous vide to cook. A wonderful "season and set aside" main dish. The lamb can stay in the sous vide overnight (or longer), so you can prepare it the day before and keep it in the water bath.

DARK CHOCOLATE BUDINO WITH SHORTBREAD CRUMBLE AND SWEET CREAM

Luxurious and rich, this Italian chocolate pudding is deceptively easy to make, and you will be stunned at how delicious and smooth it tastes. Topped with a rose-and-lavender-flecked crumble and a dollop of whipped cream. This dish can be made the day before.

LEMON GIN FLORA

• Makes one 5-ounce cocktail •

Light, citrusy, with a dreamy, floaty froth of egg white on top, this gorgeous riff on a classic gin sour is perfect for spring. I used a gin with hints of orange and rose, but any floral type of gin will work well. Garnish with early wildflowers like purple violets and apple blossoms.

Note: This cocktail uses a raw egg white to create the luxurious "foam" that is a part of traditional gin sours. If you've ever ordered a cocktail with a foamy top, it's probably been an egg white! It's perfectly safe, as long as the eggs are fresh and have remained chilled, but if egg white isn't for you, you can substitute 1 ounce (30 ml) of aquafaba (chickpea water) instead. It will froth up and mimic the egg white foam quite well.

INGREDIENTS

2 ounces (60 ml) gin with floral notes,
like The Botanist or Monkey 47

1 ounce (30 ml) fresh lemon juice

¾ ounce (23 ml) fresh Cara Cara orange juice

¾ ounce (23 ml) simple syrup (*see page 39*)

½ ounce (15 ml) elderflower liqueur

1 egg white, or aquafaba
1 ounce (30 ml)

tiny pinch of kosher salt

ice

for garnish:
edible flowers like violets, pansies, or apple blossoms

INSTRUCTIONS

1. Pour the lemon juice, orange juice, simple syrup, gin, and elderflower liqueur into ½ of a shaker.

2. Using two small bowls, crack a fresh egg and separate the white from the yolk. Add the egg white (or aquafaba) to the shaker. (The yolk is not needed for this recipe, but you can use it for something else, like the Sabayon on page 216!)

3. Add a small sprinkle of kosher salt to the cup (this heightens the citrus flavors!).

4. Scoop a generous handful of ice into the shaker cup and close.

5. Shake vigorously for 45 seconds, or until frothy.

6. Strain the cocktail into a coupe, using a Hawthorne strainer or small fine-mesh strainer.

7. Garnish with edible flowers and serve immediately.

CREAMY BASIL DIP
WITH FRESH VEGETABLES

I love starting a big meal with a light veggie-based appetizer, and this one couldn't be simpler. Using a variety of fresh vegetables, we'll arrange a platter and serve them with an addictive creamy basil-yogurt dip. Fresh, tangy, and herbaceous, this starter is wonderful for large gatherings or an impromptu cocktail hour!

Note: Modern high-speed blenders can unintentionally give a bitter aftertaste to the dressing as the oil emulsifies. The higher speed separates more-acrid phenol compounds out of the oil (where they taste neutral) and into the water-soluble portion. Try lower speeds, a lower-phenol olive oil (the most costly extra-virgin olive oils are usually highest in phenols), or pulsing rather than long high settings if you find the bitterness component too assertive.

INGREDIENTS

For the Dip

(this recipe can also be used as a delicious salad dressing)

Can be prepared up to 3 days in advance

• Makes about ½ cup (120 ml) •

1 handful (10 g) fresh basil leaves

1 tablespoon (15 g) plain Greek yogurt

1 tablespoon (15 ml) champagne vinegar

¼ cup (60 ml) olive oil

1 teaspoon (5 ml) fresh lemon juice

½ teaspoon (3.5 g) honey

½–1 full clove (2.5–5 g) fresh garlic

kosher salt and freshly ground black pepper to taste

For the Vegetable Platter

• Serves 8 •

1 cup (240 g) peeled baby carrots

6 (450 g) Persian cucumbers

1½ cups (225 g) yellow grape tomatoes

16 (450 g) mini sweet peppers

for garnish:
edible flowers such as dill flowers, fennel flowers, pansies, cosmos, or radish flowers

INSTRUCTIONS

For the Dip

1. Place the washed basil leaves, Greek yogurt, olive oil, champagne vinegar, and lemon juice in a blender.

2. Peel the garlic glove and add to the blender, along with the honey. Season with a generous pinch of salt and a few grinds of black pepper.

3. Close and blend until creamy. Adjust salt and pepper to taste.

4. Pour the dressing/dip into a small serving bowl and cover. Refrigerate for at least 15 minutes before serving.

To Assemble

1. Wash and dry the fresh vegetables and herbs.

2. Trim the ends off the Persian cucumbers. Slice lengthwise in half and then cut quarter strips from each half.

3. Taking a medium-sized platter, place the bowl of creamy basil dressing in the center.

4. Next, arrange the fresh vegetables in groups around the platter. Be creative! I like to start with the bulkier carrots and mini peppers and then fill in the spots with the rest of the vegetables. We want a lot of color and variety on the platter.

5. Garnish with your edible flowers and herbs. You don't need to follow a rigid pattern in your decorating—you can place several flowers in spots that seem to you to need a pop of color. Once you have some set as "anchors," add more flowers and herbs randomly on the platter, as though they have "fallen into place" from above.

 Replace the dairy Greek yogurt with plain unsweetened almond milk yogurt. Swap the honey in the dip for agave nectar.

CITRUS AND ROASTED BEET SALAD
WITH HONEYED VINAIGRETTE

• Serves 8 •

Beets are a beautiful balance of sweet and earthy. We'll add even more layers of flavor by roasting these deep-crimson beets with orange juice and cinnamon. Wheels of beet are interspersed with sweet-and-tart pink grapefruit and mellow Cara Cara oranges, then topped with fresh basil and a sweet honey-and-champagne vinegar dressing.

INGREDIENTS

4–5 large red beets (about 1000 g)

¼ cup (80 ml) water

¼ cup (80 ml) orange juice

1 cinnamon stick

1 large (700 g) pink grapefruit

3 (700 g) Cara Cara oranges

2 (400 g) navel oranges

1 handful (10 g) fresh Italian basil

Honeyed Vinaigrette (*see page 30*)

Substitute agave nectar for the honey in the vinaigrette.

INSTRUCTIONS

1. Preheat the oven to 375°F and reserve a 9-by-13-inch (22 × 33 cm) casserole pan.

2. Trim and wash the beets, removing any lingering dirt.

3. Using a fork, prick the beets several times. This will let the beets release steam while baking.

4. Add the water, orange juice, and cinnamon stick to the baking dish and stir lightly.

5. Place each beet into the casserole pan, larger side down, and then cover the whole pan tightly with aluminum foil.

6. Place on the center rack of the oven and roast for 1–1½ hours, or until a knife can slide into the beet easily.

7. Remove the baking dish and set on a cooling rack. Let cool to room temperature before peeling the skins off the beets.

8. Using several sheets of paper towels, gently rub the skins off all the beets. They should peel easily with a little bit of pressure. I like to wear latex gloves during this step to stop my hands from becoming stained! Discard the cooking liquid and cinnamon stick.

9. Using a sharp chef's knife, slice a small circle off the top and bottom of each grapefruit and orange.

10. Next, cut away the citrus skins along with the pith, being careful not to take too much of the fruit with it. The finished citrus should have limited white pith and be super-juicy.

11. Cut each beet and citrus piece in half from top to bottom, then slice into ¼-inch (0.5 cm) rounds. You can create one citrus wedge for each plate to use as your "backstop," and prop up the other slices if desired.

12. Using a medium-sized platter to serve family style (or salad plates to individually portion), we'll begin to layer the ingredients. Start with a citrus segment and alternate with the beets. Top with hand-torn basil and a drizzle of the Vinaigrette.

Honeyed Vinaigrette

· Makes about ¼ cup (80 ml) ·

Sweet, tangy, and slightly acidic, this is a lovely light dressing for any salad.

INGREDIENTS

4 tablespoons (60 ml) extra-virgin olive oil

2 tablespoon (30 ml) champagne vinegar

2 teaspoons (14 mg) honey

kosher salt and freshly ground black pepper to taste

INSTRUCTIONS

1. Add all the ingredients to a glass jar with a tightly fitted lid, or to a small mixing bowl.

2. Close the jar and shake vigorously to mix. If using a bowl, fork-whisk to combine.

3. Season to taste with salt and pepper.

SOUS VIDE LEG OF LAMB
WITH ROSEMARY AND MINT
• Serves 6–8 •

Tender lamb is always a treat, especially when it's seasoned with fresh mint, rosemary, and garlic. We'll be using the sous vide method, or a "water bath" style, of cooking the lamb. When you cook low and slow in a water bath, a sous vide machine is the best way to cook proteins easily and efficiently. Simply season the lamb, vacuum seal, and place in a water bath with one of these magic sous vide cylinders attached. That's it! This is a hands-off method that produces perfectly cooked restaurant-quality lamb for you and your guests!

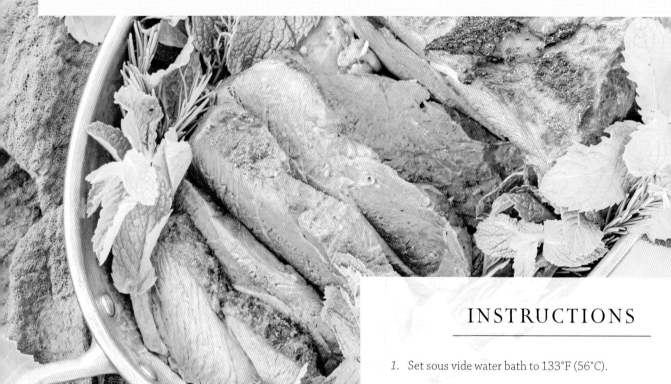

INSTRUCTIONS

1. Set sous vide water bath to 133°F (56°C).

2. Wash and pat dry the leg of lamb.

3. Open the butterflied leg and place all herbs and garlic cloves inside. Generously salt the interior of the leg, then close the butterflied segment back over the herbs.

4. Generously apply kosher salt and pepper to the exterior of the leg

5. Seal in sous-vide-safe bag and place in water bath for 8 hours (or more).

6. When the cooking time is complete, remove the leg from the bag, reserving the liquid cooking juices for a jus.

7. Broil (with the fat side up) or grill (with the fat side down) the lamb briefly (about 2–3 minutes) to render the fat and brown the outside of the leg.

8. Place the cooking juices in a small saucepan and bring to a boil. A "protein raft" will form on top of the liquid. Remove as much of this as possible with a spoon and continue to boil the liquid for an additional minute. Strain through a fine-mesh strainer and serve alongside the leg of lamb.

INGREDIENTS

1 boneless leg of lamb (about 5 pounds, or 2.25 kg)

8 sprigs of thyme

8 sprigs of rosemary

8 mint leaves

8 cloves of garlic

kosher salt, freshly ground black pepper

special equipment:

a sous vide (immersion cooker)

DARK CHOCOLATE BUDINO
WITH SHORTBREAD CRUMBLE AND WHIPPED CREAM

• Serves 6–8 •

This recipe is a chocolate lover's dream! Sinfully smooth and filled to the brim with high-quality chocolatey lusciousness. I've elevated the presentation of this Italian-style pudding with a shortbread cookie crumble infused with dried rosebud and lavender, and everything's topped with sweet whipped cream. With just a handful of ingredients, you can whip up a truly decadent dessert for your family!

INGREDIENTS

5 large (about 275 g) eggs, yolks separated from the whites

½ cup (100 g) sugar

1½ cups (360 ml) heavy cream

½ cup (120 ml) whole milk

4 ounces (115 g) semisweet baking chocolate, finely chopped

4 ounces (115 g) 60% cacao baking chocolate, finely chopped

½ teaspoon (1.5 g) kosher salt

1 teaspoon (4.8 g) vanilla extract

2 tablespoons (28 g) butter, at room temperature

Vanilla Whipped Cream (*see page 102*)

INSTRUCTIONS

1. Separate the egg yolks and the egg whites. Add the egg yolks (only) to a large mixing bowl. Discard the egg whites (or use right away in a gin sour!).

2. Add the sugar to the egg yolks and whisk until well combined.

3. Slowly whisk in the heavy cream and whole milk until incorporated.

4. Take a medium-sized pot and pour in the egg-and-cream mixture. Place the pot over medium heat and whisk. Cook low and slow until slightly steaming.

5. Add the chopped chocolate and stir with a rubber spatula until melted.

6. Continue stirring and cooking the pudding until it starts to thicken, about 8–10 minutes. You'll know it's ready when the chocolate pudding can coat the back of a spoon.

7. Remove from the heat and stir in the salt, vanilla extract, and butter until incorporated.

8. Using a fine-mesh sieve placed over a large mixing bowl, gently strain the Budino to remove any cooked egg clumps. Press the pudding through the sieve with a clean rubber spatula.

9. Portion out about 4 ounces (120 ml) of the pudding into each of 8 dessert dishes. I like to serve these in small glass dessert cups or coupe glasses, but you can use small ramekins or jam jars as well.

10. Transfer the pudding cups to the refrigerator and let chill to set for at least 2 hours. To serve, garnish with crumbled Shortbread (*see right*) around one edge, and a dollop of whipped cream.

Dried-Rosebud-and-Lavender Shortbread Cookies

Deliciously crispy and buttery, these delicate cookies are amazing crumbled on top of velvety chocolate Budino pudding, or enjoyed as a sweet treat with a cup of tea.

• Makes 18 thin cookies •

INGREDIENTS

½ teaspoon (0.5 g) edible dried rosebuds

½ teaspoon (0.5 g) edible lavender flowers

¾ cup (170 g) butter, at room temperature

½ cup (100 g) sugar

1½ cup (192 g) all-purpose flour

¼ teaspoon kosher salt

INSTRUCTIONS

1. Preheat the oven to 325°F and line a baking sheet with parchment paper.

2. Using a mortar and pestle, or a clean spice grinder, grind or pulse the rosebuds into a coarse powder.

3. In the bowl of a food processor, pulse together the butter and sugar until blended.

4. Add the flour, dried lavender flowers, and ground rosebuds to the food processor. Sprinkle in the salt. Pulse until blended.

5. Scrape the cookie dough onto the center of the parchment-lined baking sheet.

6. Using your hands, shape the cookie dough into a rough rectangle, about ¼ inch (0.5 cm) thick.

7. Bake for 12–14 minutes, or until lightly golden.

8. Remove from the oven and place the baking tray on a cooling rack. Let cool for 10 minutes. (These can be enjoyed separately from the Budino by cutting them into cookie-sized portions.)

9. Crumble and add to each Budino. Store extras in a covered container.

BLOSSOM DINNER

TABLESCAPE

Spring is in the air! Outside the window, robins are hunting for their morning breakfast, while vibrant-green crocus buds poke up through the soft earth. We will be setting a beautiful pastel-themed tablescape that is inspired by all the new life emerging around us.

COLOR

I chose an analogous color palette that is harmonious and reflects the joy of the season! Verdant greens, soft pinks, apricots, and blue-violet shades transport us to burgeoning country gardens and warm, sunny days.

BLOOMS

Lush pink peonies, roses, iris, stems of snapdragon, bright-green hosta, and playful pansies light up the scene. We'll use several large peonies as the bulk of our arrangement. Pops of color come from deep purple irises, and texture from nigella 'Baby Blue' flowers.

WHAT YOU'LL NEED

white tablecloth

linen table runner and napkins

various sturdy candlesticks and candles

neutral-colored plates and place mats

brightly colored glasses

gold-toned napkin rings

THE DETAILS

Light-green textured glass goblets and pink accent linens set the scene. Woven basket-weave place mats and neutral-colored dishware help highlight the bright palette of pastels and make the flowers pop off the table. Tall crystal and wooden candlesticks are used to hold hand-rolled beeswax pillars. Small ornamental touches are scattered around the table, including a pair of charming ceramic fox and rabbit vases, as well as several hand-blown eggshells, used as delicate flower vessels. Giant hosta leaves serve as a burst of vernal color at each setting. A large decorative vase in the shape of a classic Roman bust takes center stage, with a "crown" of heavy peonies and delicate irises.

Set the Table

Location

Any large, bright, and sunny room! If you live in a warmer climate, a three-season porch or patio is another great option.

Order of Operations

Lay your white tablecloth on the table and place a colored linen runner horizontally across the middle. Set your "anchor" items on the table first; your large centerpiece and candlesticks should be arranged center or just off-center. Begin your place settings with a place mat, followed by dinner and salad plates. Arrange your napkins and silverware at each setting.

Small Touches

This is where you get to add your own personal details. I've placed a large hosta leaf on top of each salad plate, as well as colored-glass goblets and water glasses. Blown-out eggshells filled with pansies are spaced around the centerpiece, secured on napkin rings. Additional flowers are spread across the table. Think of small touches that say "spring" to you.

BLOSSOM DINNER

GIN AND GREEN TEA

A delightful cocktail of gin and chilled green tea that is both floral and refreshing. The delicate floral notes of elderflower liqueur help amplify the flavors of the herbaceous gin and the leafy flavors of the green tea.

GARLIC AIOLI WITH BLANCHED EARLY-SPRING GARDEN VEGETABLES

A buttery garlic and olive oil emulsion, this classic European dip is delicious when paired with blanched early-spring vegetables, like asparagus, radishes, sugar snap peas, and baby potatoes. The aioli can be made the day before.

MOZZARELLA PESTO TOASTS WITH CRISPY PANCETTA AND PICKLED RHUBARB

Gourmet toasts aren't just for breakfast! This hearty dish is creamy, crunchy, and savory, all at once. Fancy toasts are a wonderful vehicle for seasonal ingredients and can be a creative appetizer idea for any party.

POTATO RICOTTA GNOCCHI WITH LEMON AND GREEN PEAS

These tender and pillowy gnocchi will be sure to delight your guests! This homemade pasta recipe is easy to make, and just delicious. Soft on the inside, and pan-fried to a golden brown on the outside, the gnocchi are then tossed in an easy white wine and lemon sauce. The raw gnocchi dough can be prepared in advance and frozen to save time.

FLOURLESS CHOCOLATE ESPRESSO CAKE WITH EDIBLE FLOWERS

Flourless chocolate cake is an impressive dessert for any occasion. A beautiful contrast of dense, almost brownie-like inner crumb and pillowy clouds of whipped cream on top. This cake can be made the day before if needed, but the whipped cream will lose its texture after an hour or so.

GIN AND GREEN TEA

• Makes two 4-ounce cocktails •

A sophisticated take on a classic gin cocktail, this green-tea-infused gin sour recipe is perfect for the tea lover, the gin lover, or the cocktail lover. Light, bright, and so refreshing!

Note: This is also a wonderful recipe to scale up as a batch cocktail. Serve in a pitcher or glass beverage dispenser.

INGREDIENTS

3 ounces (90 ml) green tea, freshly brewed and chilled

1 ounce (30 ml) freshly squeezed lemon juice

1 ounce (30 ml) Basic Cocktail Simple Syrup (*see right*)

2 ounces (60 ml) gin with herbaceous notes, such as Hendrick's Gin

½ ounce (15 ml) elderflower liqueur

ice

INSTRUCTIONS

1. Pour the green tea, lemon juice, gin, elderflower liqueur, and simple syrup into the cup of a cocktail shaker.

2. Add a generous scoop of ice and close the shaker. Vigorously shake until chilled, about 30 seconds. The outside of the shaker should be lightly frosted when ready.

3. Using a cocktail strainer, pour the cocktail into 2 coupe glasses.

4. Enjoy chilled.

Basic Cocktail Simple Syrup

The easiest and simplest syrup recipe. I always have a batch on hand in my refrigerator, for all of my cocktail making. It's also convenient to use to sweeten iced tea and lemonade recipes.

• Makes about 1 cup (240 ml) •

INGREDIENTS

1 cup (240 ml) water

1 cup (200 g) sugar

INSTRUCTIONS

1. Add the sugar and water into a medium-sized pot. Stir.

2. Place over medium-high heat and bring to a boil.

3. Let boil for 5 minutes, until all of the sugar has dissolved.

4. Remove from the heat and let cool slightly.

5. Store in a glass jar with a tightly fitted lid. Refrigerate for up to 2 weeks.

GARLIC AIOLI

• Serves 6–8 •

WITH BLANCHED EARLY-SPRING GARDEN VEGETABLES

With recipe roots throughout France, Spain, and Italy, this versatile olive oil spread can be slathered on practically anything! Similar to a mayonnaise in texture, this variation uses a hefty dose of garlic and fresh lemon juice. Dried mustard and fresh tarragon add a lovely savory note. Served with blanched spring vegetables and boiled eggs, this recipe is excellent as an appetizer or light meal.

Note: Modern high-speed blenders can give a bitter aftertaste to the dressing as the oil emulsifies. Try lower speeds, a low-phenol olive oil, or pulsing, rather than long, high spins, to minimize bitterness.

INGREDIENTS

For the Garlic Aioli

3 cloves (15 g) garlic, finely minced

2 fresh eggs (about 110 g)

1 tablespoon (15 ml) freshly squeezed lemon juice

¼ teaspoon (6 g) mustard powder

1½ cups (360 ml) high-quality extra-virgin olive oil

1 tablespoon (5 g) fresh tarragon, minced

kosher salt and freshly ground black pepper to taste

For Blanching the Spring Vegetables and Boiling the Eggs

4 cups (1 L) water

5 pounds (680 g) baby potatoes (I like to use a medley of yellow, purple, and red potatoes)

16 ounces (450 g) fresh radishes

1 pound (450 g) fresh asparagus spears

4 ounces (115 g) sugar snap peas

4 large eggs (about 220 g)

kosher salt

for garnish:

edible fresh flowers such as pansies, alyssum flowers, fennel flowers, chive blossoms, and dianthus; flaky finishing salt (optional)

INSTRUCTIONS

For the Garlic Aioli

1. Peel and finely mince the garlic. This will help homogenize the garlic faster and reduce overall blending time.

2. In 2 small bowls, separate the eggs. One bowl for the egg whites and the other bowl for the egg yolks. Reserve the egg yolks and discard the egg whites.

3. In a large mixing bowl or blender at low to medium speed, whisk together the egg yolks, minced garlic, mustard powder, and lemon juice and a small pinch of salt until combined.

4. Next, while whisking or blending on low speed, slowly drizzle in the olive oil. We are creating an emulsion. The sauce will transform from loose and oily to a viscous creamy sauce that's a rich yellow in color.

5. Add the minced tarragon. Mix.

6. Season to taste with salt and freshly ground black pepper.

For the Spring Vegetables and Boiled Eggs

1. Wash and dry the vegetables and potatoes. Trim the stems off the radishes and cut off the lower third of the asparagus spears. Remove the stems and strings from the sugar snap peas.

2. Using a medium-sized pot, add the 4 eggs and 2 cups (480 ml) of water. Sprinkle in ½ teaspoon (5 g) kosher salt.

3. Place over medium-high heat and bring to a bowl. Let boil for 8 minutes. In the meantime, take a large mixing bowl and add equal parts ice and water. This is an ice bath for the eggs.

4. After 8 minutes, remove the eggs from the boiling water and place into the ice bath. Let cool completely. Discard the cold water. Peel by cracking the eggs on the counter and, using a spoon, peel the eggs under cold running water.

5. Using a large shallow pot, add 3 cups (500–700 ml) of water and a generous pinch of salt. Add the potatoes and place the pot over medium-high heat.

6. Bring to a boil and cook the potatoes until tender, 10–15 minutes.

7. While waiting for the potatoes to cook, prepare a fresh ice bath in a large mixing bowl.

8. Once the potatoes are soft, scoop them out of the boiling water with a slotted spoon and transfer them to the ice bath to quickly stop the cooking. Keep the pot of boiling water on medium-high heat and add more water if it boils down too low.

9. Once the potatoes are cool, remove from the ice bath to a small bowl.

10. Working in batches, you'll blanch the remaining vegetables; boil the sugar snap peas for 1 minute and remove to the ice bath with a set of tongs, boil the asparagus spears for 3 minutes and remove with tongs to the ice bath, then boil the radishes for 2 minutes and place in the ice bath. Let cool completely. Refill ice as needed.

To Assemble

Use a large platter or cheese board to arrange the ingredients.

1. Place a small serving bowl of the garlic aioli in the center or upper corner of the platter.

2. Next, add the asparagus spears in small bundles.

3. Halve the baby potatoes, boiled eggs, and radishes with a sharp knife. Arrange on the board.

4. Place the snap peas where you want to add color.

5. Dot the edible fresh-flower garnish around the whole board or platter.

6. Finish with a quick sprinkle of finishing salt on the boiled eggs and potatoes.

7. Serve chilled.

MOZZARELLA PESTO TOASTS
WITH CRISPY PANCETTA AND PICKLED RHUBARB

• Serves 8 •

"Fancy toasts" have always been in fashion, whether it's the iconic avocado toast or the good old-fashioned sunny-side-up egg and cheese on bread. One of my favorite variations is this one, featuring homemade pesto on toasted sourdough bread, topped with slices of creamy mozzarella, sliced grape tomatoes, crispy pieces of pancetta, and little pops of tart pickled rhubarb. Drizzled with a fresh chive oil, the combination is savory, salty, tart, and sweet. Every bite is the perfect one!

INGREDIENTS

8 slices sourdough bread

¼ cup (60 ml) + 2 tablespoons (30 ml)
extra-virgin olive oil, divided

¼ cup (20 g) chives, roughly chopped

4 ounces (115 g) yellow or red grape tomatoes

4 ounces (115 g) diced pancetta

16 ounces (450 g) fresh mozzarella

kosher salt

freshly ground black pepper

1 batch of Quick-Pickled Rhubarb (*see page 44*)

1 batch of Basil Pine Nut Pesto (*see page 44*)

for garnish:

microgreens such as onion sprouts, arugula, or radish; fresh
edible flowers such as pansies, chive flowers, or basil flowers

To Assemble

1. Reserve a platter or large cutting board for serving.

2. Add a generous dollop of pesto to each toast and spread evenly.

3. Next, layer 2–3 slices of fresh mozzarella on each toast.

4. Add several slices of tomato, a sprinkle of the pancetta, and about a tablespoon of the rhubarb (*see page 44*).

5. Assemble all the toasts onto a platter.

6. Finish by drizzling the toasts with the chive oil, and garnish with fresh microgreens and edible flowers.

INSTRUCTIONS

1. Set the oven to low broil.

2. Place the slices of sourdough bread on a large baking sheet and arrange so there is space between them.

3. Using a silicone pastry brush or a rubber spatula, spread the 2 tablespoons (30 ml) of extra-virgin olive oil on both sides of the bread slices. Return to the baking pan.

4. Place the baking sheet on the middle rack of the oven and broil the bread until golden brown. About 3 minutes per side. After toasting, place on a cooling rack.

5. Add the remaining ¼ cup (60 ml) of extra-virgin olive oil to the jar of a blender, along with the chives and a small pinch of kosher salt. Add a few grinds of fresh black pepper. Close and blend until incorporated. Pour the finished chive oil into a small bowl.

6. Heat a large skillet to medium high and add the diced pancetta. Cook until crispy and rendered. Drain the pancetta on a plate with paper towels.

7. Wash and dry the tomatoes. Slice into thin ⅛-inch (0.25 cm) rounds.

8. Slice the mozzarella into ¼-inch (0.5 cm) rounds.

 Use gluten-free sourdough bread.

QUICK-PICKLED RHUBARB

• Makes two 16-ounce (500 ml) pint jars •

Quick-pickling is an age-old tradition, and easier than you think. Simply create a hot brine and add to your fruits or vegetables. I've created this spring pickle mixture with a combination of fresh rhubarb, red strawberries, shallots, and dried lavender buds. The result? These pickled fruits and vegetables turn out spicy, sweet, and tart, with a hint of floral notes.

INGREDIENTS

1 pound (450 g) fresh rhubarb

1 cup (160 g) fresh strawberries

1 large (80 g) shallot

1½ cups (360 ml) water

¾ cup (180 ml) apple cider vinegar

2 tablespoons (18 g) kosher salt

1 tablespoon (7 g) whole black peppercorns

1 teaspoon (1 g) edible dried lavender buds

special equipment: 2 sterilized glass pint jars and lids

INSTRUCTIONS

1. Wash and dry the rhubarb stalks and strawberries.

2. Cut the ends off the rhubarb stalks and then cut each stalk into 4-inch-long (10 cm) sections. Trim the tops off the strawberries and cut into quarters. Peel the shallot and slice into thin rings.

3. Taking the sanitized jars, begin to pack them with stalks of rhubarb, pieces of strawberries, and rings of shallot. Stand the rhubarb pieces up lengthwise in the jars and add the other ingredients around them.

4. In a small pot, add the water, apple cider vinegar, kosher salt, black peppercorns, and dried lavender buds and bring to a boil.

5. Once boiling, remove from the heat and allow to cool slightly before ladling the hot pickling liquid into each jar, stopping about 1 inch (2.5 cm) from the top.

6. Close tightly and let cool to room temperature. The jar lids will "pop" as the temperature drops, creating a natural vacuum seal.

7. Place in the refrigerator for at least 2 days before using.

Note: These pickled fruits are good for at least 2 weeks if kept chilled.

Basil Pine Nut Pesto

A zippy blend of fresh basil, olive oil, pine nuts, and garlic. This flavorful fusion can be used as a marinade, sauce, or spread. It's delicious with meats, fish, or vegetables, or even as a potato topping.

• Makes 1 cup (240 ml) •

INGREDIENTS

2 ounces (60 g) fresh basil

½ cup (60 g) pine nuts

½ cup (120 ml) extra-virgin olive oil

2 cloves (10 g) garlic, peeled and minced

kosher salt and freshly ground black pepper to taste

INSTRUCTIONS

1. Using a food processor, add all the ingredients into the food processor bowl. Close tightly and pulse to blend. Periodically pause and scrape down the sides with a rubber spatula.

2. Blend fully for just about 1 minute, or until smooth.

3. Add salt and black pepper to taste.

4. Store in a covered container in the refrigerator for up to 3 days.

POTATO AND RICOTTA GNOCCHI
WITH LEMON AND GREEN PEAS · Serves 8 ·

Pillowy-soft potato gnocchi require just a handful of humble ingredients and create a beautiful fresh pasta. Quickly boiled and then toasted golden brown in sizzling butter, these gnocchi will be accompanied by a quick white wine and lemon pan sauce. Finally, everything is topped with fresh lemon zest, tender pea shoots, and plenty of garden herbs. This is the pasta dish you've been waiting for!

Note: Uncooked, shaped gnocchi freezes very well. This recipe makes quite a bit of pasta, so freezing an uncooked batch is handy for future meals. To freeze, set the cut and shaped gnocchi on a baking tray in the freezer and transfer to a bag or covered container once frozen solid.

INGREDIENTS

For the Pasta

2 large russet potatoes (500 g), peeled and cubed

1 tablespoon (15 ml) + 2 teaspoons (10 ml) extra-virgin olive oil, divided

¾ cup (100 g) all-purpose flour + more for rolling

1 egg (55 g)

¼ cup (60 g) ricotta cheese

3 tablespoons (15 g) fresh chives, minced

½ teaspoon (1.5 g) kosher salt

¼ teaspoon (0.4 g) freshly ground black pepper

4 cups (1 L) water

1 tablespoon (14 g) butter

special tools: potato ricer

INSTRUCTIONS

1. Prepare a large pasta pot filled halfway with water, and place on high heat. Add a big pinch of kosher salt and bring to a boil.

2. On a large cutting board or counter, sprinkle a little bit of the flour to keep the dough from sticking to the surface.

3. Place the peeled and cubed potatoes in a microwave-safe bowl. Add enough water to just barely cover the bottom of the potatoes. Cover and cook in the microwave for 10 minutes on high (if cooking on the stovetop instead, add enough water to cover the tops of the potatoes and cook on medium-high heat until soft).

4. Drain the potatoes and pat dry. Using a potato ricer, "rice" the potatoes directly onto the work surface (the gnocchi may have lumps if the potato isn't evenly mashed, so a ricer is the right tool for the job!).

5. Take a medium-sized fine-mesh sieve or flour sifter and sift ¾ cup (100 g) flour directly over the mound of riced potato.

6. Next, make a small well in the middle of the potatoes with your finger. Scramble an egg in a small bowl with a fork and pour into the well.

7. Add the chopped ricotta cheese, chives, kosher salt, and freshly ground black pepper to the well.

8. Before forming the pasta dough, be sure to have some extra flour on hand, in case the dough becomes too sticky.

9. Taking the potato-and-flour mixture from the outside to the inside, gently fold from the outside edges into the well. Repeat this step until the egg and ricotta are just incorporated. If the dough feels wet and sticky, add 1–2 tablespoons of flour. Remember: less is more when adding the flour. It is important not to overwork this dough or the gnocchi will be chewy instead of pillowy, so try to have the ingredients just incorporated.

10. Once you've folded the dough until just smooth, form it into a rough circle. Cut the circle in half and wrap one piece in plastic (unless you're making a boatload of gnocchi!). You can store this extra dough in the fridge for a day or so, or longer in the freezer.

11. Cut the dough in half again and choose a piece to work with. With floured hands, begin to roll the dough into a snake. You want it to be about as thick as your thumb. You can pinch a piece of the dough off if you don't have a wide surface to work with.

12. Take a knife and cut the individual gnocchi into shape, each about 1 inch (2.5 cm) long. Place the gnocchi on a clean plate. Repeat with the next quarter of dough.

13. After cutting, gently press a divot into each gnocchi with your finger. The dent will help the gnocchi hold the sauce.

To Cook

Note: If you're cooking this as you read, please check the sauce recipe on the next page—start the sauce before boiling the pasta, then toss in the ¼ cup of pasta water (for the starches) right before you add the gnocchi.

1. Ensure your large pot, with 4 cups (1 L) of water, is at a low boil, and prepare a sieve (or slotted spoon) to scoop up the cooked pasta from the water.

2. Heat a large skillet with 1 tablespoon (14 g) of butter and 1 tablespoon (15 ml) of olive oil.

3. Working in small batches, place your gnocchi into the pot of boiling water and cook for 90 seconds, or until they all float.

4. Once the gnocchi are floating, remove the pasta with a sieve or slotted spoon, drain well, and place directly into the hot skillet. Fry the gnocchi on both sides until golden brown, about 3 minutes per side. Set gnocchi aside and repeat steps 2–5 until the desired amount of pasta is cooked.

5. Transfer the gnocchi into the sauce (*see next page*) to finish in the pan.

GREEN PEA AND LEMON WHITE WINE SAUCE

• Serves 8 •

Light and lemony, this quick pan sauce is delicious with fresh gnocchi, or any pasta you have on hand!

INGREDIENTS

½ cup (70 g) frozen peas
(we will blanch these, then shock them in ice water)

2 tablespoons (28 g) butter

1 tablespoon (15 ml) extra-virgin olive oil

3 cloves (15 g) garlic, minced

1 large (80 g) shallot, minced

1 lemon, zested + 1 teaspoon (15 ml) fresh lemon juice

¼ cup (80 ml) white wine

¼ cup (80 ml) vegetable or chicken stock

¼ cup (80 ml) reserved gnocchi pasta water

kosher salt and freshly ground black pepper

1 cup (10 g) fresh basil, torn

3 tablespoons (15 g) finely grated Parmigiano Reggiano cheese

for garnish: 1 ounce (30 g) organic pea shoots and
1 ounce (30 g) organic onion sprouts

INSTRUCTIONS

1. Prepare a pot of boiling water (you can use your boiling pasta water) as well as an ice bath (a large bowl with water and ice).

2. Place the peas in a small sieve and submerge (still in the sieve, so they don't escape!) in the boiling pasta water for 1 minute. The peas will turn a bright-green color as they cook. After 1 minute, remove the peas from the boiling water and quickly "shock" them by transferring to an ice bath. This will immediately stop the cooking process and maintain the vibrant color of the peas.

3. Place a large skillet on medium heat. Once hot, add the butter and olive oil. Let cook until the butter is slightly foamy.

4. Add the garlic, shallots, ½ teaspoon (1.6 g) lemon zest, a pinch (about 1.2 g) of kosher salt, and freshly ground black pepper. Stir occasionally and allow to cook down until the shallots become slightly translucent, about 6 minutes.

5. Pour the white wine, vegetable stock, and lemon juice into the skillet. Add ¼ cup (80 ml) of the "used" pasta water. We will use the natural starches released from cooking of the pasta to help thicken the sauce.

6. Allow the sauce to come to a low boil and slightly thicken.

7. Add the pan-seared gnocchi and the peas to the sauce. Stir or toss to coat completely.

8. Remove from the heat, add the hand-torn basil leaves, and stir. Adjust the salt and black pepper to taste.

To Plate

1. Transfer the contents of the pan to a large serving dish.

2. Garnish with Parmigiano Reggiano cheese, lots of fresh lemon zest, and microgreens.

3. Serve immediately.

FLOURLESS CHOCOLATE ESPRESSO CAKE WITH EDIBLE FLOWERS

· Serves 8–10 ·

In my mind, it's not truly a dinner party until you get to dessert! Whether it's light and airy or dense and sweet, I think of desserts as the make-or-break dishes for any event. My Flourless Chocolate Espresso Cake with Edible Flowers will make your guests gasp with delight. Decadent chocolate with an espresso finish, for a match made in heaven.

INGREDIENTS

6 tablespoons (85 g) salted butter + extra for greasing the pan, cold and cubed

8 ounces (225 g) 60% cacao bittersweet baking chocolate

6 large (about 330 g) eggs, separated into yolks and whites

½ cup (100 g) sugar

2 tablespoons (12 g) espresso powder

1 tablespoon (13 g) vanilla sugar (or substitute 1 teaspoon [4.8 g] vanilla extract)

to top: Vanilla Whipped Cream (*see page 102*)

to garnish: fresh edible flowers such as pansies and violets, plus fresh raspberries.

special equipment:
9-inch (23 cm) springform pan

INSTRUCTIONS

1. Preheat the oven to 275°F (this type of cake bakes best at a lower temperature because of the egg-white base) and place a rack in the middle position.

2. Prepare the springform pan; cut a circle of parchment paper to fit the inner section of the pan, and insert. Grease the edges, and the parchment paper, with about a tablespoon of butter.

3. Roughly chop the bittersweet baking chocolate. Add to a large microwave-safe bowl, along with the cubed salted butter. Melt the butter and chocolate together in the microwave in 30-second intervals, on high heat. Stir with a fork between each heating. Melt until smooth (about 4 intervals). Let cool slightly.

4. Separate your eggs into two separate bowls: one containing the yolks and the other the egg whites.

5. Next, whisk the egg yolks into the melted chocolate mixture until combined. Add the espresso powder to the chocolate and mix until incorporated (if using vanilla extract instead of vanilla sugar, add now as well).

6. In the bowl of a stand mixer, using the whisk attachment (or using a handheld mixer and a large bowl), beat the egg whites on high until soft peaks are formed. The egg whites should look white instead of translucent, and when you pick some up on a spoon, the tip should still flop over. This is often called a "soft peak" when beating egg whites.

7. Lower the mixer to medium speed and gradually add the regular sugar to the egg whites. Return to high speed and beat until "stiff peaks" are formed. Stiff peaks look glossy and white. You can test the stiffness by lifting a dollop of the beaten egg white and sugar on a spoon; the egg whites should stand straight and tall (no "flopping over" of the tip).

8. Take ¼ of the egg whites and whisk into the chocolate / egg yolk mixture from step 5.

9. Using a rubber spatula, fold the remaining stiff egg whites into the chocolate batter. You want most of the egg whites to mix into the chocolate, but don't mix so vigorously that the airiness of the beaten egg whites dissolves completely.

10. Next, using a spatula, gently scrape the batter into the prepared springform pan. Lightly spread and smooth out the top.

11. Bake for 45 minutes. The cake will rise significantly but then fall quite a bit after you remove it from the oven. The top will have a gorgeous cracked surface.

12. Cool completely on a wire rack before serving.

13. Remove from the springform pan and transfer (carefully!) to a cake plate or cake stand, using two sturdy spatulas. The parchment paper should help create a stronger base.

14. Top the flourless cake with clouds of vanilla whipped cream and raspberries and garnish with edible flowers.

MOTHER'S DAY BRUNCH

FRESH GRAPEFRUIT APEROL SPRITZ

A bright and rosy bubbly drink to celebrate Mom on her special day! With just a few ingredients, this is a brilliantly simple cocktail to serve for brunch.

BLUEBERRY GOAT CHEESE SALAD
WITH CREAMY BASIL DRESSING

Salads can be deceptive in their simplicity! The key to making a great salad stand out on a menu is to incorporate lots of different textures and tastes. This recipe does the trick! We've hit all of the high notes with tart berries, creamy goat cheese, crunchy vegetables, and my favorite creamy basil dressing. The basil dressing can be made up to two days in advance.

BLUEBERRY GRANOLA FRENCH TOAST
WITH EARL GREY CRÈME ANGLAISE

I think everyone gets excited when French toast is on the menu! It's important to start with the best base; dense brioche is soaked in a sweet custard and then quickly cooked in butter. We'll add layers of flavor with a batch of homemade coconut-almond granola, fresh blueberries, and an Earl Grey crème anglaise. This is a breakfast that will really wow Mom!

ASPARAGUS AND SMOKED GOUDA
CRUSTLESS QUICHE

This savory and smoky dish is packed with flavor, and such an elegant way to serve eggs! Even better? You can save time and make this dish a bit in advance and serve hot or at room temperature. This dish can be made the day before and reheated.

MINI SUGAR COOKIE LEMON TARTS

Adorable daisy and tulip-shaped sugar cookie tart shells are filled with sunny fresh lemon curd. As delicious as they are pretty, they pair beautifully with our table's colorful macarons. I've topped them with a dollop of whipped cream and a sprinkle of pansies. The cookies and lemon curd can be made separately the day before and assembled the day of your event.

FRESH GRAPEFRUIT APEROL SPRITZ

• Makes 1 generous drink •

The orange flavor of Aperol, an Italian aperitif (a fortified liqueur), is very distinct. By itself, its bitter notes predominate, with hints of rhubarb, burnt orange, and an almost fresh green herblike quality. To sweeten and balance an aperitif, it is usually paired with other components. This recipe blends it with fresh pink grapefruit juice in a variation of a classic Aperol spritz. Refreshing, bubbly, and with just the perfect amount of sweetness, this is a great drink to share over brunch.

INGREDIENTS

4 ounces (120 ml) prosecco or champagne

3 ounces (90 ml) Aperol liqueur

2 ounces (60 ml) freshly squeezed pink grapefruit juice

1 ounce (30 ml) soda water

½ teaspoon (7.5 ml) simple syrup

ice

for garnish:
grapefruit slices and edible flowers, such as fresh lavender sprigs and red dianthus

INSTRUCTIONS

1. Fill a large wine glass with ice.

2. Layer in the prosecco (or champagne, Aperol, and pink grapefruit juice)

3. Add the simple syrup and soda water. Mix gently with a cocktail spoon (a chopstick also works!).

4. Garnish with grapefruit slices and edible flowers.

BLUEBERRY GOAT CHEESE SALAD
WITH CREAMY BASIL DRESSING · Serves 8 ·

This lovely blue-and-green salad is an amazing starter for any meal, and I think my favorite plate of greens ever. In my mind, a great salad has to meet these four elements: color (in this case, bright greens and colorful fruits), texture (here supplied by crunchy nuts and creamy cheese), flavor (always a mix of sweet/bitter/salty/sweet), and indulgence (the rich salad dressing and creamy avocado). I have to say, this recipe hits all the marks for me!

INGREDIENTS

6 cups (180 g) mixed baby greens

4 (500 g) Persian cucumbers

2 (400 g) ripe avocados

¾ cup (130 g) fresh blueberries

8 ounces (225 g) creamy goat cheese

½ cup (60 g) raw pepitas (pumpkin seeds)

Creamy Basil Dressing (*see page 28*)

INSTRUCTIONS

1. Wash and dry all the vegetables and the blueberries.

2. Using 8 salad plates (or serve family-style, on 1 large platter), add the greens as a base.

3. Trim the ends off the Persian cucumbers and slice into ¼-inch (0.5 cm) round pieces. Divide equally among the plates.

4. Next, halve the avocado around the pit along its longer axis, separate, and scoop out the insides. Using a sharp knife, cut the avocado into ¼-inch (0.5 cm) slices. Arrange on top of the salad in a loose fan shape.

5. Scatter the blueberries on top of the greens and add 1 ounce (30 g) of goat cheese in dollops.

6. Top each plate with 1 tablespoon (7.5 g) of pepitas and drizzle with the Creamy Basil Dressing.

BLUEBERRY GRANOLA FRENCH TOAST

WITH EARL GREY CRÈME ANGLAISE

French toast is such a versatile breakfast dish, and I couldn't help but go all out. The dense brioche bread pairs beautifully with this vanilla-flavored custard, and the oven-baked coconut-almond granola adds even more sweetness and texture. Instead of syrup, the tea-infused crème anglaise brings a unique luxuriousness to the plate, while a tangy crème fraîche whipped cream balances everything with a touch of tart. The beauty of this dish is that whether you can use all of these additions, or just a few, you're going to have a delicious experience!

INGREDIENTS

1 large loaf of brioche-style bread (or challah), sliced into 12 thick pieces

1½ cups (360 ml) whole milk

2 tablespoons (60 ml) heavy whipping cream

3 eggs (about 160 g)

2 teaspoons (9.6 g) vanilla extract

2 tablespoons (25 g) sugar

¼ teaspoon (0.6 g) ground cinnamon

1 cup (170 g) fresh blueberries

4 tablespoons (60 g) butter, for frying

Additions:

Coconut-Almond Granola (*see page 56*)

Earl Grey Crème Anglaise (*see page 54*)

Crème Fraîche Whipped Cream (*see page 56*)

for garnish:

freeze-dried blueberries (crushed), edible flowers such as wild violets, borage, or purple pansies

INSTRUCTIONS

1. Slice the bread into 12 thick pieces.

2. In a large mixing bowl, whisk together the milk, cream, eggs, and vanilla extract. Next, whisk in the sugar and cinnamon.

3. Heat a large nonstick skillet over medium-high heat with a tablespoon of butter. Allow the butter to get foamy, but be careful not to burn it!

4. Dip two slices of brioche into the custard, pushing it under the surface to make sure both sides are coated properly. Brioche is great at absorbing the eggy custard, so a few seconds for each side will be enough here! Once it is dipped and coated for a few seconds on each side, place the bread into the hot pan and cook for 3–4 minutes on each side, or until golden brown.

5. Repeat with all of the bread slices, adding butter to the pan as needed.

To Serve

1. Place one piece of French toast on a plate and scatter a handful of fresh blueberries on top, followed by 2 tablespoons of the granola. Drizzle with the crème anglaise and then repeat the berries–granola–crème anglaise layers.

2. Finish with the crème fraiche whipped cream dolloped around the plate, and optionally a sprinkle of crushed freeze-dried blueberries. Garnish with edible flowers.

Earl Grey Crème Anglaise

An elegant tea-infused custard sauce for cake, fruit, or French toast.

• Makes about 2 cups (480 ml) •

INGREDIENTS

1½ cups (360 ml) whole milk

1 bag (3 g) Earl Grey tea

1 teaspoon (4.8 g) vanilla extract

¼ cup (50 g) granulated sugar

6 egg yolks

INSTRUCTIONS

1. Pour the milk into a medium-sized pot and place over medium heat. Submerge the bag of Earl Grey tea in the milk and heat until steaming. Stir occasionally, being careful not to scald the milk by overcooking.

2. After heating, remove the tea/milk mixture from the stove and gently press the tea bag down with a spatula before discarding.

3. In a large bowl, whisk the sugar and egg yolks together until blended.

4. To temper the eggs, slowly ladle in ¼ cup of the hot tea/milk in a thin stream while whisking the sugar and egg mixture. Slowly add the hot tea/milk to gently warm the eggs and prevent curdling. Continue to slowly ladle the milk mixture into the eggs, until about half the milk is incorporated. Keep whisking!

5. Pour the egg mixture into the remaining tea/milk in the pot, while continuing to whisk. Turn the heat to medium and keep stirring with a rubber spatula.. Watch that the liquid doesn't cook too quickly and create a "skin" on top, while using slow, constant heat.

6. Continue stirring until the liquid thickens enough to coat the back of the spatula. Remove from the heat and stir in the vanilla extract.

7. Using a fine-mesh sieve placed over a storage container, strain the custard for any leftover egg curd.

8. Cover the custard (if using plastic wrap, press right onto the surface of the custard to prevent a film from forming as it chills) and keep refrigerated until use.

Small-Batch Coconut-Almond Granola

This gluten-free granola is delicious on top of French toast but also adds great texture to a bowl of yogurt or ice cream. You can also treat it like a cereal and eat it with milk!

· Makes about 1 cup (240 g) ·

INGREDIENTS

1½ cups (120 g) old-fashioned rolled oats

½ cup (60 g) slivered almonds

¼ cup (30 g) unsweetened coconut flakes

¼ cup (30 g) raw pumpkin seeds

2 tablespoons (30 ml) vegetable oil

2 tablespoons (42 g) honey

1 tablespoon (7.5 g) brown sugar

1 teaspoon (4.8 g) vanilla extract

½ teaspoon (1.5 g) kosher salt

¼ teaspoon (0.6 g) ground cinnamon

INSTRUCTIONS

1. Preheat the oven to 350°F and line a large baking sheet with parchment paper.

2. In a large mixing bowl, combine all the ingredients and stir well. The texture will be a little bit "clumpy."

3. Spread the granola in one even layer onto the baking sheet and bake for 20–24 minutes, or until just golden.

4. Cool completely on a wire rack and transfer to an airtight container. It can be stored for up to 2 weeks.

Crème Fraîche Whipped Cream

Sweet, but not too sweet, this tangy whipped cream has an almost yogurt-like flavor from the crème fraîche. If crème fraîche isn't available at your local grocery store, you can use an equal amount of regular sour cream instead.

· Makes 12 servings ·

INGREDIENTS

¾ cup (180 ml) heavy whipping cream

¼ cup (60 g) crème fraîche

¼ cup (32 g) confectioners' sugar

½ teaspoon (2.4 g) vanilla extract

1 pinch (about 1.2 g) kosher salt

INSTRUCTIONS

1. In the bowl of a stand mixer with a whisk attachment, or using a handheld mixer, add the heavy cream and crème fraîche. Whip on medium high, until just thickened.

2. Pause the mixer and add the confectioners' sugar, vanilla, and salt.

3. Continue to whip on medium high, until medium peaks are achieved.

4. Keep chilled until use. Serve dolloped or piped onto the plate.

ASPARAGUS AND SMOKED GOUDA CRUSTLESS QUICHE

• Serves 8 •

This quiche will get you loads of compliments when served for brunch, or even for dinner! We'll forgo the traditional crust and keep this recipe simple. The beauty of this quiche is that it is simple to put together, and delicious whether hot or at room temperature. The combination of fresh green vegetables with the smoky cheese and cured bacon makes this an easy hit.

INGREDIENTS

10 spears asparagus, washed, and the bottom ⅓ trimmed off

2 cloves (10 g) fresh garlic, peeled and finely minced

2 shallots (180 g), peeled and sliced into ¼-inch (0.5 cm) rings

10 ounces (280 g) frozen spinach, cooked and drained well

6 ounces (170 g) smoked gouda, shredded

6 large (about 330 g) eggs

1 cup (240 ml) whole milk

1 cup (240 ml) half-and-half or light cream

¼ teaspoon (0.75 g) kosher salt

¼ teaspoon (0.4 g) freshly ground black pepper

½ teaspoon (1.6 g) smoked paprika

4–6 slices thick-cut bacon

½ tablespoon (7 g) butter, for greasing the baking dish

INSTRUCTIONS

1. Preheat the oven to 350°F and lightly butter a 10.5-by-7.5-inch (27 × 20 cm) baking dish.

2. Roughly chop asparagus spears into about ½-inch-long (1 cm) pieces. Set aside with the prepared garlic, shallots, and spinach. Shred the gouda.

3. Place a large skillet over medium-high heat. Take the thick-cut bacon and slice thinly into strips (lardons), about ¼ inches (0.5 cm) in width.

4. Add the lardons to the hot pan and cook until rendered and crispy. Once cooked, place the lardons on a paper-towel-covered plate.

5. In the same skillet, sauté the chopped asparagus, spinach, minced garlic, and sliced shallots. Stir frequently, cooking for about 5 minutes or until the asparagus turns a bright-green color.

6. Beat the eggs, milk, cream, and seasonings together in a large bowl. Slowly pour the egg mixture into the skillet with the sauteed vegetables, returning the lardons as well. Slowly cook the mixture, while stirring with a spatula, until loose egg curds start to form. You do not want to fully scramble the eggs.

7. Sprinkle on the shredded cheese and quickly stir for about a minute to incorporate.

8. Scrape the quiche mixture into the prepared casserole dish and bake for 30 minutes, or until firm and golden brown.

9. Once cooked, remove from the oven to a cooling rack and let stand 10 minutes before serving.

MINI SUGAR COOKIE LEMON TARTS

• Makes 4 dozen cookies •

Let's celebrate spring with a classic dessert, reimagined! Daisy-and tulip-shaped sugar cookie crusts filled with a zippy homemade lemon curd creates the perfect whimsical dessert for your party. Topped with homemade whipped cream and edible flowers, these cookie tarts are great for Mother's Day, baby showers, or afternoon tea!

INGREDIENTS

For the Cookie Tart Shells

1 cup (230 g) butter + 1 tablespoon more to grease the pan, cool to the touch but not cold

1 cup (200 g) sugar

1 egg (about 55 g)

1 tablespoon (15 g) vanilla extract

3 teaspoons (10 g) lemon zest

1 fresh lemon, juiced (about 30 ml juice)

2 teaspoons (9 g) baking powder

3 cups (385 g) all-purpose flour

¼ teaspoon (1.5 g) kosher salt

special equipment:

1 large (for the daisy cup) and 1 medium (for the tulip cup) flower-shaped cookie cutters

1 mini-tart-baking pan

6–8 small stainless-steel condiment cups

piping bags

assorted frosting tips (optional)

For the Lemon Curd

½ cup (100 g) + ¼ cup (50 g) sugar, divided

½ cup freshly squeezed lemon juice (120 ml juice, or about 4 lemons)

1 tablespoon (10 g) fresh lemon zest

3 eggs (about 165 g), room temperature

¾ cup (170 g) butter, at room temperature

for garnish: Vanilla Whipped Cream (*see page 102*) and edible fresh flowers, such as wild violets, pansies, johnny jump-ups, and cherry blossoms

Replace the all-purpose flour with *Bob's Red Mill Gluten Free 1-to-1 Baking Flour.* This is one of my favorite products to bake gluten-free cookies and brownies.

INSTRUCTIONS

For the Cookie Tart Shells

1. In a stand mixer, using the paddle, beat together the butter and sugar until creamed (about 5 minutes on medium-high speed).

2. Add the egg, vanilla extract, lemon zest, and lemon juice to the mixer bowl. Continue to mix until combined.

3. Scrape down the mixer bowl with a rubber spatula and beat in the baking powder, salt, and flour. Add the flour in 2–3 batches until incorporated.

4. Lay out 2 sheets of plastic wrap and transfer the batter into the center. With your hands, form a rough circle of dough and wrap tightly with plastic wrap. Chill for at least 1 hour before baking.

5. After chilling, place the cookie dough on the counter to rest for 15 minutes.

To Bake

1. Preheat the oven to 350°F. Lightly grease the mini tart pan with butter for the daisy-shaped cookies. For the tulip-shaped cookies, line a baking sheet with parchment and grease 6–8 oven-safe mini metal sauce bowls. Flip them upside down and arrange on the baking sheet. These will be the "third dimension" for your tulip cookies.

2. Flour your countertop or a large cutting board (you can also use a piece of wax paper instead). Working in small batches, cut an inch-wide (2.5 cm) slice from your circle of cookie dough.

3. Gently roll out your dough to about ¼ inch (0.5 cm) thick. This is thin enough to be a good tart shell, but not so thin that it will burn in the oven.

4. Using the larger flower-shaped cookie cutter, cut out several daisy-shaped flowers and place in the cups of the mini tart pan. Using the medium-sized flower-shaped cookie cutter, cut several slightly smaller "tulips" and drape over the inverted mini metal sauce bowls.

5. Using the back of a tablespoon or the bottom part of a small sauce bowl, gently create a "bowl" by pressing down on the center of each "daisy" cookie in the mini tart pan. This small dent will help the cookie tart hold the curd after baking.

6. Fork-prick a few venting holes at the bottom of the "daisy bowl," as well as on the bottoms of the tulip-shaped cookies. Place the pans in the refrigerator for 5 minutes to firm up. Chilling just a little bit before baking really helps the cookies maintain their shape while in the oven.

7. Bake for 10–12 minutes, or until the edges turn golden brown.

8. Allow the cookies to cool in the pan (or on the condiment cups) on a wire rack for about 5 minutes. Then, gently twist the flower cookies from the molds and cool completely.

9. Repeat the process until you have the desired number of cookies.

For the Lemon Curd

1. In a medium saucepan, add the lemon juice, lemon zest, and ½ cup (100 g) of sugar, whisking to combine. Set over medium heat and bring to a boil, whisking occasionally. This will create a lemon syrup.

2. Once the syrup reaches a low boil, remove from the heat.

3. In a medium mixing bowl, whisk the eggs and the ¼ cup (50 g) of sugar until combined. The eggs and sugar should be completely incorporated and almost smooth in texture.

4. To temper the egg mixture: using a ladle, slowly pour a thin stream of the still-hot lemon syrup into the egg mixture, while whisking continuously. This action will warm the eggs slowly and avoid any scrambled egg curds.

5. Continue to pour in the lemon syrup in a thin stream, whisking continuously, until ⅓ of the simple syrup is incorporated.

6. After combining ⅓ of the syrup into the egg mixture, pour the entire bowl back into the medium saucepan, fully combining the lemon syrup with the eggs and sugar. Bring to a slow boil on medium heat while whisking. The liquid will begin to thicken after about 8 minutes.

7. After you've reached a low bubbling boil, continue whisking for an additional minute. The curd will begin to look like a viscous hollandaise sauce.

8. Remove from the heat and let cool for 1 minute.

9. Slowly add the butter 1 chunk at a time, using a spatula to stir gently until each chunk is completely melted and incorporated.

To Assemble

1. Add the lemon curd to a piping bag and twist to close. Add the whipped cream to a second piping bag (this one fitted with a medium-sized, star-shaped, stainless-steel piping tip if available). Twist to close.

2. Snip the corner off the lemon curd piping bag with a pair of kitchen scissors. Holding the piping bag firmly, begin to squeeze the lemon curd into the cookie tart crusts. We want to fill the daisy-shaped cookie tart crusts about ¾ of the way full, while the tulip-shaped ones are about halfway filled.

3. Continue filling until you have the required number of mini tarts.

4. Next, top off each tart with the desired amount of whipped cream from the piping bag. Feel free to get creative! You can pipe on 1 large rosette or place several smaller ones on each tart.

5. Garnish with edible fresh flowers. I like to add 1–2 to each tart.

6. Refrigerate until serving.

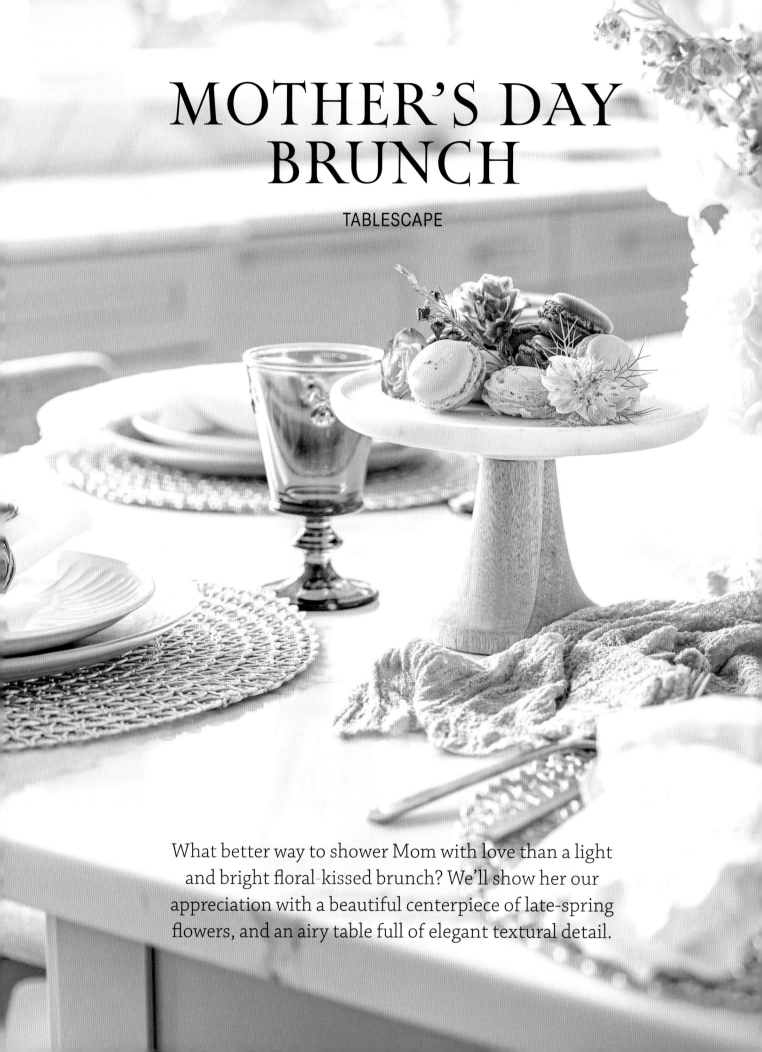

MOTHER'S DAY BRUNCH

TABLESCAPE

What better way to shower Mom with love than a light and bright floral-kissed brunch? We'll show her our appreciation with a beautiful centerpiece of late-spring flowers, and an airy table full of elegant textural detail.

COLOR

We will be using a color palette made principally of analogous bright pinks and blues, with a contrasting blend of creamy white. Golden-yellow decorative pieces help create more visual interest and elevate this table.

BLOOMS

Bright-pink peonies, white hydrangea, deep-purple iris, lavender gillyflower, and nigella 'Baby Blue' flowers are arranged into a loosely spherical form. I've used a simple blown-glass vase for this bouquet.

THE DETAILS

To create something that was elegant, but not fussy, for this Mother's Day tablescape I focused on a few key elements, including our beautiful floral centerpiece, combined with heavier painted wooden candlesticks with white pillar candles, and a vintage white milk-glass bowl filled with fresh lemons. To soften the scene, I used small feminine touches, with embroidered napkins and a small marble cake stand of pastel French macarons.

64

WHAT YOU'LL NEED

light-blue linen table runner or cloth

light-colored woven place mats

deep-blue dinner plates

off-white textured salad plates

blue drinking glasses

doily-esque cotton napkins

gold-toned napkin rings

heavy wooden candlesticks with pillar candles

Set the Table

Location

A kitchen table, or large kitchen island.

Order of Operations

Drape your runner across the length of the table or counter. Add your floral centerpiece, the fruit bowl, and the wooden candlesticks. Arrange your table settings and place the doily napkins into holders before setting at each place. Set the gold-toned decorative objects throughout.

Small Details

I've added extra floral touches by slipping a lavender-colored gillyflower into each napkin ring, as well as garnishing the cake stand with additional flowers. Gold decorative accents such as spheres, figurines, or small objects d'art; a decorative bowl with fresh citrus; and a small cake stand with French macarons add pops of color and vibrancy to the table. The macarons, or any colorful sweet you prefer, can be purchased or baked at home. There is no rule about what you might want to buy versus bake to add a bit of color to your table!

"BUILD A BOUQUET" BABY SHOWER

HOMEMADE BLUEBERRY LEMONADE

There's nothing like a freshly squeezed glass of cold lemonade! I've created a flavored version with homemade blueberry simple syrup for extra pizazz. Refreshing and alcohol-free. The blueberry simple syrup can be made up to a week in advance, and the lemonade base can be made the day before.

BAKED FETA IN PHYLLO DOUGH
WITH THYME-INFUSED HONEY

Both salty and sweet, this recipe uses feta slices that are then baked in a flaky phyllo "package." Drizzled with a homemade thyme-scented honey and finished with juicy mixed berries.

TANGY CUCUMBER AND DILL SALAD

My variation on a traditional eastern European cold cucumber salad. Crunchy cucumbers are mixed together with a vibrant combination of red onion, mint, and fresh dill for a refreshing spring salad course. Tossed together with a tangy red-wine vinegar and yogurt dressing. The yogurt dressing can be made the day before.

SAVORY TURKEY MEATBALLS WITH ROASTED
BALSAMIC TOMATOES AND CELERY ROOT PUREE

This is an elegant dish that will knock your guests' socks off. Herb-and-panko-infused ground turkey meatballs are baked in the oven, then paired with cherry tomatoes roasted with brown sugar and balsamic vinegar. Served over an incredibly velvety celery root puree. The tomato sauce can be made the day before, but the meatballs and puree will be best if made the day of your event.

SWEET NECTARINE CAKE WITH WHIPPED
VANILLA BUTTERCREAM FROSTING

Juicy nectarines and layers of tender yogurt vanilla cake—what more could you ask for? Frosted with a light vanilla buttercream and garnished with a garden's worth of edible flowers. This rustic-looking cake makes decorating a breeze! It can be made the day before your event and stored in the refrigerator.

HOMEMADE BLUEBERRY LEMONADE

• Makes 8 servings •

This drink is made for warm spring days! I've added a juicy berry flavor to the fresh lemonade base with a blueberry-infused simple syrup. Because the simple syrup is denser than the lemonade itself, it can be placed at the bottom of the glass to create a gorgeous gradient effect, until you give it a quick stir! Made by the glass, or by the pitcher, this is a beautiful nonalcoholic beverage for your next gathering.

INGREDIENTS

For the Blueberry Simple Syrup

½ cup (85 g) fresh blueberries

1 cup (200 g) sugar

1 cup (240 ml) water

For the Lemonade

1½ cups (360 ml) fresh lemon juice (about 8 large lemons)

3 cups (720 ml) filtered cold water

1 cup (240 ml) + more to taste, Blueberry Simple Syrup

ice

for garnish:
fresh sprigs of mint, lavender flowers,
and wild violets

INSTRUCTIONS

To Make the Blueberry Simple Syrup

1. Combine the sugar, blueberries, and water in a medium-sized saucepan. Place the pot on high heat. Stir occasionally to dissolve the sugar while heating.

2. Bring the mixture to a low boil. Cook for 8 minutes, while stirring occasionally.

3. When it has thickened to a jammy texture, remove from the heat. Gently press the blueberries with a potato masher or fork to release all the fruit juices. Let cool slightly.

4. Using a fine-mesh sieve placed over a bowl, strain the syrup while pressing down on the solids with a spoon or rubber spatula. This will release any extra juices. Discard the solids.

5. Store the blueberry simple syrup in a glass jar with a tightly fitting lid. Chill until use.

6. This syrup will keep for up to 2 weeks in the refrigerator.

To Make the Lemonade

1. Juice the lemons and add to a large pitcher. Pour in the 3 cups (750 ml) of cold water and stir.

2. For a pitcher: Add 1 cup of the blueberry simple syrup to the lemonade base and stir well. Taste and adjust the sweetness by adding more syrup as desired. Fill the pitcher halfway with ice and enjoy!

3. For individual servings: Using tall Collins glasses, add 3 tablespoons (45 ml) of the blueberry syrup per glass. Fill each glass about ¾ full of ice. Slowly pour in the lemonade base. The drink will have a wonderful violet color gradient. Garnish with edible flowers and fresh mint. Don't forget to stir your drink before enjoying—the sweetness is at the bottom! :)

BAKED FETA IN PHYLLO DOUGH
WITH THYME-INFUSED HONEY · Serves 8 ·

Salty, sweet, creamy, and crunchy. These are the hallmarks of a great starter! This dish builds those features by wrapping a slice of feta cheese in delicate phyllo dough and baking to a golden brown. Served by drizzling with warmed honey infused with fresh thyme. If you can, garnish with fresh lavender sprigs, since the flavor and aroma will pair gorgeously with the dish!

INGREDIENTS

1 cup (330 g) + 2 teaspoons (28 g) local honey, divided

3–4 sprigs fresh thyme

8 ounces (225 g) medium-hardness feta cheese

5 sheets phyllo dough

1 tablespoon (15 ml) extra-virgin olive oil

½ cup (80 g) fresh strawberries

¼ cup (40 g) fresh blueberries

¼ cup (40 g) fresh raspberries

2 teaspoons (10 ml) orange juice

1 empty tea bag or tea ball (to hold the thyme for
easier retrieval—optional)

for garnish:
edible fresh lavender sprigs and geranium flowers

INSTRUCTIONS

1. Preheat the oven to 350°F and prepare a baking tray with a large piece of parchment paper. Allow the feta and phyllo dough to come to room temperature.

2. Combine the honey and thyme sprigs into a small saucepan and place over low to medium heat (I like to place my thyme sprigs in an empty tea bag to steep in the honey, for convenience).

3. Let the honey warm, but not cook, for 10 minutes. Remove from the heat and let sit for another 5 minutes. Discard the thyme tea bag or strain the honey into a sieve over a glass jar, to catch the thyme leaves and stems.

4. Cut the feta cheese into slices a little less than 1 inch (about 2 cm) thick.

5. Carefully unfold the phyllo dough and gently layer 5 sheets of phyllo on top of the parchment-covered baking sheet. I like to place each sheet at slightly different angle than the last, to create more texture.

6. Place a slice of feta in the middle of the phyllo sheets. Using a silicone pastry brush or rubber spatula, brush olive oil onto the outer inch (2.5 cm) of the phyllo dough edges.

7. Gently fold the left-hand side of the phyllo dough over the center, followed by the top portion, right side, and bottom. Flip the entire "package" over, seam side down, on the baking sheet.

8. Brush the remaining oil over the top and sides of the phyllo dough. Place into the oven and bake for 25–30 minutes, or until golden and flaky. Repeat the whole process with the second slice of feta cheese.

9. While the feta bakes, prepare the berries. Wash and dry all the berries, destem and halve the strawberries, then mix all berries in a bowl and add the 2 teaspoons (14 g) of honey and 2 teaspoons (10 ml) of orange juice, Mix gently and let the berries rest.

10. Once the feta has baked, transfer to a cutting board and slice into halves or quarters, at your preference.

11. To plate, place the cheese semistacked on a small platter. Top with the berries and generously drizzle with thyme-infused honey. Garnish with fresh lavender sprigs and edible geranium flowers.

TANGY CUCUMBER AND DILL SALAD

• Serves 8–10 •

Filled with fresh and fragrant herbs and crunchy cucumbers, here's a refreshing side! Crisp and cool cucumbers are the star of the show, highlighted by the flavors of red onion, dill, mint, and chives. Topped with a pleasantly acidic dressing of fresh lemon, red wine vinegar, and Greek yogurt, with a hint of red chili.

INGREDIENTS

2 large English cucumbers, peeled (about 700 g)

¼ (50 g) large red onion

3 tablespoons (15 g) minced fresh chives

½ bunch (40 g) fresh dill + extra to garnish

2 sprigs fresh mint, leaves stripped from the stems

½ cup (115 g) plain Greek yogurt

1 tablespoon (13 g) mayonnaise

1 tablespoon (15 ml) red wine vinegar

2 teaspoons (10 ml) fresh lemon juice

½ teaspoon (0.8 g) dried red pepper flakes

½ teaspoon (1.5 g) kosher salt

¼ teaspoon (0.4 g) freshly ground black pepper

for garnish: ½ cup (75 g) halved cherry tomatoes, onion sprouts, clover sprouts, dill flowers, geranium flowers

INSTRUCTIONS

1. Trim the ends off the peeled cucumbers, cut down the middle lengthwise, and then again, quartering the cucumber into a spear. Cut each spear into ¼-inch pieces and add to a large mixing bowl.

2. Thinly chop the red onion and add to the bowl along with the minced chives. Hand-tear the mint leaves and add to the bowl (hand tearing prevents the mint leaves from discoloring due to contact with the steel knife). Roughly chop the fresh dill and remove any woody stems. Add to the bowl.

3. Next, add the plain Greek yogurt, mayonnaise, red wine vinegar, and lemon juice to the bowl. Season with the salt, black pepper, and chili flakes.

4. Mix well with a large spoon. Adjust the salt and black pepper to taste.

5. Cover the bowl with plastic wrap and let chill for 15 minutes.

6. Transfer to a serving bowl or plate individually. Garnish with more fresh dill, dill flowers, or geranium flowers.

SAVORY TURKEY MEATBALLS WITH
ROASTED BALSAMIC TOMATOES AND CELERY ROOT PUREE

• Serves 4–6 (double or triple the recipe for a large crowd) •

This is a delicious and simple recipe to prepare, elevated by gorgeous plating. Humble ingredients like ground turkey, tomatoes, and knobby celery root are transformed into a gourmet plate worthy of any party! Slow-roasted tomatoes with brown sugar and balsamic vinegar, poured over moist turkey meatballs, all sitting on a bed of ultrasmooth pureed celery root.

INGREDIENTS

For the Roasted Cherry Tomato Sauce

18 ounces (500 g) cherry tomatoes

3 cloves (15 g) garlic, peeled and finely minced

¼ cup (80 ml) extra-virgin olive oil

1 tablespoon (15 ml) white wine vinegar

2 teaspoons (10 ml) aged balsamic vinegar

1 tablespoon (7.5 g) light brown sugar

1 handful (10 g) fresh basil leaves + more for garnish, torn

generous pinch (about 2 g) kosher salt

generous pinch (about 1 g) fresh ground pepper

For the Celery Root Puree

1 medium celery root (about 750 g)

3 cups (720 ml) water

3 tablespoons (42 g) butter

¼ cup (80 ml) heavy cream

generous pinch (about 2 g) kosher salt

GF Replace the panko breadcrumbs with your favorite gluten-free version, as well as using a gluten-free balsamic vinegar for the roasted tomato sauce.

71

For the Turkey Meatballs

16 ounces (450 g) 85% lean unseasoned ground turkey

⅓ cup (20 g) plain panko breadcrumbs

1 egg (about 55 g)

2 tablespoons (10 g) finely grated Parmigiano Reggiano cheese + more for garnish

1 large (80 g) shallot, peeled and minced

2 cloves (10 g) garlic, peeled and finely minced

1½ teaspoons (4.5 g) kosher salt

1 teaspoon (0.8 g) dried oregano

½ teaspoon (0.8 g) dried chili flakes

¼ teaspoon (0.8 g) smoked paprika

INSTRUCTIONS

To Make the Roasted Tomato Sauce

1. Preheat the oven to 325°F and reserve a 9-by-13-inch (22 × 33 cm) baking dish.

2. Wash the cherry tomatoes and place half into a large mixing bowl. Cut the remaining tomatoes in half and add to the bowl. (Keeping some of the tomatoes whole will create a little texture variation and stop your sauce from getting too watery.)

3. Add the minced garlic, olive oil, vinegars, brown sugar, torn fresh basil, salt, and pepper. Stir to combine.

4. Add the tomatoes to the baking dish and spread them out slightly. Roast in the oven for 50–60 minutes, until bubbly and cooked down. The tomatoes will slightly caramelize and release their juices. After baking, remove the dish from the oven and place on a wire rack.

For the Celery Root Puree

1. Slice the root side off the celery root and then peel the tough outer skin off with a vegetable peeler or knife. Cut the peeled root in half, then cut again into medium-sized cubes.

2. Fill a large pot halfway (3 or so cups, 720 ml) with cold water and a large pinch of kosher salt. Add your celery root chunks to the pot on medium-high heat and let boil. Once at a boil, cook until fork tender (similar to potatoes), about 20 minutes.

3. Once soft, drain the celery root chunks in a colander and transfer them into a blender with 3 tablespoons (42 g) butter, ¼ cup (80 ml) cream, and a pinch of kosher salt.

4. Cover and blend until smooth. Unlike potato, this puree will not become "gluey," but if the puree is very thick, add a splash more heavy cream.

5. Place a fine-mesh sieve over a medium-sized bowl. Add the puree into the sieve and gently press through with a rubber spatula. This will give you the perfect velvety texture.

6. Adjust the salt if needed.

For the Meatballs

1. Preheat the oven to 375°F. Line a large baking sheet with a piece of parchment paper.

2. In a large mixing bowl, add the ground turkey, panko, egg, Parmigiano Reggiano cheese, garlic, shallot, and spices to the bowl. Mix together with your hands to thoroughly combine.

3. Using a gentle touch, scoop a small handful (about 2 tablespoons) of the meat mixture and lightly roll it in your hands. Use only a little bit of pressure to roll the ground turkey mix together—we want to make nice, soft meatballs!

4. Place the raw meatballs about 1½ inches apart on the parchment-covered baking sheet. You should be able to make 8–12 meatballs from this recipe.

5. Bake at 375°F for 20 minutes, or until the meatballs reach an internal temperature of 165°F.

To Assemble

1. Using a shallow pasta bowl, place two heaping spoonfuls of celery root puree at the bottom of the bowl and spread slightly with the back of a spoon. Next, add two meatballs on top. Generously spoon the roasted tomato sauce over the meatballs. Garnish with fresh basil and thin shavings of Parmigiano-Reggiano.

SWEET NECTARINE CAKE
WITH WHIPPED VANILLA BUTTERCREAM FROSTING

• Serves 10–12 •

When you're throwing a big celebratory party, sometimes only a fancy cake will do for dessert! This recipe produces a rustic, yet beautiful, flower-festooned layer cake. Two layers of vanilla yogurt cake are separated by a cooked peach compote and topped with whipped vanilla buttercream frosting. Easy to make and even easier to eat! Garnished with a slight dusting of matcha green tea powder, and lots (LOTS) of fresh edible flowers, this cake is a dream.

INGREDIENTS

For the Cake

1 stick (115 g) unsalted butter + more to grease the pans, at room temperature

1 cup (200 g) sugar

2 eggs (about 110 g), at room temperature

1½ teaspoons (7.2 g) vanilla extract

1 teaspoon (3.2 g) lemon zest

1 cup (225 g) plain Greek yogurt

2 cups (256 g) all-purpose flour

1 teaspoon (4.5 g) baking soda

1 teaspoon (4.5 g) baking powder

¼ teaspoon (0.7 g) kosher salt

For the Nectarine Filling

3 slightly soft nectarines (about 400 g)

¼ cup (50 g) sugar

2 tablespoons (30 ml) water

2 teaspoons (10 ml) fresh lemon juice

For the Whipped
Vanilla Buttercream Frosting

4–5 cups (600 g) confectioners sugar, sifted

3 sticks (350 g) butter, at room temperature

2 teaspoons (10 g) vanilla extract

4 tablespoons (60 ml) heavy cream

 Replace the all-purpose flour with *Bob's Red Mill Gluten Free 1-to-1 Baking Flour.*

for garnish:

matcha green tea powder; edible flowers such as bee balm, wild violets, zinnias, pansies, marigolds, cosmos, borage, petite roses, and scented geraniums

special equipment:

2 9-inch (23 cm) cake pans

2 plastic disposable piping bags

large "sultan" piping tip

medium to large "ribbon" piping tip

offset spatula

1 10-inch (25 cm) cake board

INSTRUCTIONS

For the Cake

1. Preheat the oven to 350°F and line two 9-inch (23 cm) cake pans with round pieces of parchment paper. Grease the sides of the pans with a bit of soft butter.

2. In the bowl of a stand mixer with the paddle attachment, cream together the butter with the sugar on medium-high speed for 5 minutes. The butter and sugar should become smooth and very yellow.

3. As the butter and sugar are creaming in the mixer, add all the dry ingredients to a separate large mixing bowl: the flour, baking soda, baking powder, and salt. Fork-mix.

4. After creaming the butter and sugar for 5 minutes, beat the eggs in one at a time, until incorporated. Pause the mixer and scrape down the sides of the bowl with a rubber spatula as needed.

5. Lower the mixer speed and add in the vanilla extract, lemon zest, and Greek yogurt. Blend completely.

6. Lower the mixer speed to low medium and, in two batches, add the dry ingredients to the loose batter and blend completely (for about 3 minutes).

7. With a ladle, portion out the batter equally between the two prepared baking pans. For extra accuracy, use an electronic kitchen scale to ensure equal portions between the two pans. Smooth the top of the cake batter with an offset spatula.

8. Bake in a preheated oven for 25 minutes, or until a toothpick comes out clean from the center of each cake.

9. Remove from the oven and place the cake pans on a cooling rack for 10 minutes.

10. After cooling, carefully invert the cakes by placing a dinner plate on top of each pan and flipping the pan upside down. The cake should pop out easily. Place the cake round back on the cooling rack to cool completely.

For the Nectarine Filling

1. Wash and dry the nectarines. Cut the fruit away from the pit and roughly chop. Add the chopped fruit, sugar, water, and lemon juice to a medium-sized pot on high heat and bring to a low boil.

2. Let the mixture boil until thick and jammy, about 7–10 minutes.

3. Remove from the heat and, using a large spoon or potato masher, gently mash the mixture to create a more even consistency. Let cool completely and store in a small covered container. Chill until use.

For the Whipped Vanilla Buttercream Frosting

1. Sift the confectioners' sugar into a small bowl.

2. In a stand mixer with the paddle attachment, on medium-high speed, beat the butter for 5–7 minutes. When smooth, mix in the vanilla extract and salt.

3. Lower the mixer speed to low and slowly add the sifted confectioners' sugar in several batches. Once the confectioners' sugar is beaten in, add the heavy cream in a slow stream.

4. Beat until creamy and slightly fluffy.

To Assemble

1. About 15 minutes before you want to assemble the cake, place the cake layers into the freezer to firm them up. This helps cut down on the number of crumbs that come off when frosting.

2. Fill one piping bag halfway with frosting. No tip is needed.

3. Take the small cake board (a small paper base for cakes) and place on a regular or revolving cake stand. With an offset spatula or rubber spatula, take a spoonful of frosting and add to the middle of the cake board. Spread slightly. The frosting will help the cake stick to the board while you're assembling.

4. Take the cake rounds out of the freezer and unwrap. Trim any rough edges with a sharp paring knife. This case is "rustic," and so this step doesn't have to be extremely precise.

5. Place the first cake layer on the center of the board, with the flat (bottom) side down.

6. Spread about ½ cup (120 ml) of frosting in one even layer on the top of the cake round. Trim the tip off the piping bag filled with frosting, and pipe around the edge of the cake (above the base layer of frosting). The filling will be placed inside this "dam" to prevent the nectarine filling from leaking out between the layers of cake.

7. Spoon on between ¼ cup (80 g) to ⅓ cup (110 g) of nectarine filling and spread evenly, staying within the piped border.

8. Carefully place the next cake round on top, flat side up, and press down slightly to adhere.

9. Use a small amount of frosting to spread over the top and sides of the cake with an offset spatula or rubber spatula. It doesn't have to be thick or look perfect. This is called the *crumb coat*, a protective layer of frosting to create a barrier between the cake and the outer decorations.

10. Once the crumb coat is applied, place the whole cake into the refrigerator to cool slightly, for about 15 minutes. Return the leftover frosting to the refrigerator as well.

11. When ready to decorate, pull the cake and the frosting out of the refrigerator. Add a cup or so (250 ml) of the frosting to the top of the cake and slowly smooth from the center to the outside edges, using an offset spatula (or regular spatula). Next, add dollops of frosting to the sides and work around with the offset spatula. You can keep the cake rustic looking or smooth the top and sides with a metal bench scraper.

12. If you want to decorate with the frosting, rather than just cover the cake, fill up two piping bags halfway with frosting: one fitted with a "ribbon" tip, and the other with a "sultan" tip. Start with the "ribbon" tip and draw abstract lines off-center on top and down the sides of the cake. You can also add "branches" off the main line. Using the "sultan" tip, pipe circular shapes in bunches of 3–5 around the sides and top of the cake.

13. Optionally, you can dust portions (or all) of the cake with matcha green tea powder, dusting the top by using a small fine-mesh sieve.

14. Arrange your edible flowers on the cake. Place them beside the lines or in the circular frosting shapes; the sky's the limit!

15. Carefully transfer the cake to a covered cake plate and refrigerate until serving.

16. If making the day before, frost and pipe as above but wait until shortly before your event to dust and add the flowers.

"BUILD A BOUQUET"

BABY SHOWER

TABLESCAPE

I'm going to cut down on the stress of planning an amazing baby shower by showing you how to create both a beautiful tablescape AND a great flower-themed activity to celebrate the mother-to-be!

COLOR

We will be using an analogous palette featuring a variety of soft pinks, peaches, blue purples, and whites. If you know the gender of the expected bundle of joy and like the color tradition, you could easily stick to either pink or blue, but I love the diversity of color in this table!

BLOOMS

peonies, roses, spray roses, catmint, heather, delphinium, and white veronica 'Smart Luna'

WHAT YOU'LL NEED

ivory-colored dishware

pink linen napkins

pink-and-blue linen table runners

woven jute rope place mats

gold-toned napkin rings

pink glassware

2 galvanized buckets

5–6 jam jars in varying heights

THE DETAILS

Rustic jute rope place mats bring a textural feel, contrasting with the ivory dishware. Shades of pink and blue, through the use of linens and drinking glasses, add a lighter touch to the scene. We will use a series of small jam-jar floral arrangements, along with two large galvanized steel buckets filled with cut flowers, which will also double as flower stations, for guests to arrange their own take-home bouquets.

Set the Table

Location

A kitchen, back porch, or patio with a large surface to eat and work on.

Order of Operations

Drape the pink-and-blue runner down the length of the table or counter you're using. Set the galvanized buckets with flowers on one end of the table, along with several pairs of clippers. Place the jam jars filled with our floral arrangements down the center of the table, on top of the linen runners. Place the place mats with the ivory dishware, as well as the napkins and glassware.

Small Details

I've added several spools of rough silk ribbon in our color palette, between the flower arrangements. Not only does this give texture to the scene, but it's useful to wrap our finished bouquets! The ivory plates also have an added flourish in the form of small flutes around the edges. This is a lovely detail that draws the eye to the setting. Clippers and ribbon for guests to make their bouquets, and extra flowers, are props that will be used during the party.

Summer

The garden is ripe with greens, tomatoes, and plump summer berries. Long days and warm afternoon sunshine always inspire me to host outdoor dinners and gatherings filled with food, family, and fun! Cold, tall glasses of blueberry lemonade and bright summer salads call you to the table . . . playful parties and cookouts share space with elegant floral summer soirées—summer is the season to entertain and enjoy everything the garden has to offer!

MENUS

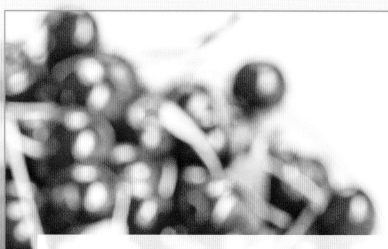

FATHER'S DAY PICNIC

FROZEN MELON-BALL SLUSHIES

Refreshing and juicy, this is a fun summer cocktail, and a much-needed momentary escape from the heat of summer. You'll love the luscious melon flavor that comes through in this vibrant drink. Serve these as an ideal icy refresher for those hot summer afternoons by the grill.

BAKED MAC AND CHEESE WITH CRISPY CORNFLAKE TOPPING

A rich and creamy bite with every forkful. Perfectly cooked pasta paired with the smooth, garlicky cheese sauce makes this dish a satisfying dinner on its own, but it also makes a wonderful accompaniment to the protein-rich salad on this menu. The mac and cheese can be made in advance and frozen if desired.

GRILLED STEAK SALAD WITH SEASONED RYE BREAD CROUTONS

A savory steak salad recipe with loads of textures, tastes, and color. When the days are hot and muggy, I sometimes just crave a crisp salad and quick hit of protein. For me, this dish hits all the notes in the key of summer. The croutons can be made the day before if needed.

LOADED OATMEAL COOKIE ICE CREAM SANDWICHES

A childhood favorite reimagined. The oatmeal cookie is the sweet hero of the dish, stuffed as it is with raisins, chocolate, and oats. The crispy outside and chewy inside pairs with any ice cream flavor you throw at it! The cookies can be made the day before if desired.

FROZEN MELON-BALL SLUSHIES

Freshly juiced honeydew melon is mixed with Midori, premium vodka, lime juice, and a quick splash of orange juice. Toss in some ice, blend on high, and you'll get the most delicious batch drink to help you stay cool in the summer sun!

INGREDIENTS

4 ounces (120 ml) juiced honeydew melon
(it's best to blend this separately; see below)

2 ounces (60 ml) Midori melon liqueur

2 ounces (60 ml) vodka

1 ounce (30 ml) lime juice

1 ounce (30 ml) orange juice

1 ounce (30 ml) simple syrup (*see page 39*)

1 cup (130 g) ice

INSTRUCTIONS

For the Melon Juice

Juicing the melon ahead of time and then straining it will give you a smoother drink.

1. Remove the skin and cube about a half of a honeydew melon (discard the seeds), then place in a blender with about ½ inch (1 cm) of water at the bottom (so as to not stall the blender with a lack of liquid).

2. Blend on high until smooth, then strain through a mesh strainer into a large bowl, pressing down with a spatula to separate the solids from the juice. Transfer the strained honeydew juice to a large jar and chill until use.

For the Cocktail

1. Place all the liquids into a blender and add 1 cup (130 g) of ice.

2. Blend on high, until foamy. You can use the "frozen drink" function, if available on your blender.

3. Pour into 2 lowball glasses.

4. Garnish with a lime wedge or pieces of melon.

BAKED MAC AND CHEESE
WITH CRISPY CORNFLAKE TOPPING
• Serves 10–12 •

Get ready for the perfect picnic side! Fun, corkscrew-shaped cavatappi pasta is combined with a creamy, traditional bechamel, loaded with cheddar cheese and gruyere. The crispy cornflake topping adds a beautiful crunch once this dish is baked to perfection!

 Swap out the regular pasta for your favorite gluten-free spiral pasta. Replace the all-purpose flour in the roux with 4 tablespoons (32 g) of ground arrowroot powder. You can leave out the traditional cornflake cereal topping or utilize an organic gluten-free version found in your local natural-foods store.

INGREDIENTS

16 ounces (450 g) dry cavatappi
(also called cellentani, depending on the brand) pasta

4 ounces (115 g) salted butter

2 large shallots (160 g), minced

2–3 cloves garlic (12 g), minced

½ cup (64 g) all-purpose flour

3 cups (730 g) whole milk

12 ounces (340 g) gruyere, shredded

8 ounces (225 g) mild cheddar, shredded

½ teaspoon (1.1 g) dry ground mustard powder

salt and ground black pepper to taste

1 cup (30 g) cornflakes, crushed

2 tablespoons (30 g) salted butter, melted
(for the cornflakes)

INSTRUCTIONS

1. Preheat the oven to 350°F.

2. Prepare the dry pasta according to the package directions, usually about 11 minutes to boil. Drain and reserve.

3. Take a large pot or Dutch oven, add the butter, and place over medium heat. Melt until foamy. Be careful not to brown the butter!

4. Add the shallot and garlic and stir. Cook until slightly softened and fragrant.

5. Sprinkle in the flour and stir in with a whisk. This will create a roux. Cook the roux until the flour turns slightly brown and smells nutty (3–4 minutes).

6. Once the roux is cooked, slowly add the milk while whisking (you want to make sure there are no clumps). The sauce will start to thicken as it heats. Continue whisking and heating until the sauce reaches a low boil.

7. Add about ¼ of the shredded cheese and mix until smooth, repeating until all the cheese is incorporated. We want a smooth and creamy sauce for our pasta.

8. After the cheese has been smoothly incorporated, add the dry mustard, salt, and pepper. Taste the sauce (careful—it's hot!) and add salt and pepper to your liking.

9. Add the pasta to the pot of cheese sauce. Stir to combine. Pour into a 9-by-13-inch (22 × 33 cm) baking dish.

10. Crush the cornflakes with your hands in a small bowl. Add the 2 tablespoons (30 g) of melted butter and stir with a spoon. Sprinkle the topping evenly over the macaroni and cheese in the baking dish.

11. Place your baking dish on the middle rack and bake for 30 minutes.

12. Remove from the oven and let rest on a wire cooling rack for 5 minutes. Serve and enjoy!

GRILLED STEAK SALAD
WITH SEASONED RYE BREAD CROUTONS

• Serves 6–8 •

Smoky and savory, this easy summer main dish features grilled flank steak over a bed of tender greens, fresh tomatoes, cucumbers, and grilled purple onions. Everything gets topped off with a batch of crunchy homemade rye croutons, and a zippy white wine vinegar and mustard dressing.

INGREDIENTS

4 slices unseeded rye bread

2 tablespoons (30 ml) extra virgin olive oil
+ 1 teaspoon (5 ml), divided

1 teaspoon (3 g) kosher salt

1 teaspoon (3.8 g) garlic powder

½ teaspoon (1.6 g) onion powder

½ teaspoon (1.6 g) smoked paprika

¼ teaspoon (0.4 g) freshly ground
black pepper

1 tablespoon (5 g) shredded
Parmigiano-Reggiano

16 ounces (450 g) flank steak,
or cut of your choosing

1 head of butter lettuce

1 cup (150 g) cherry tomatoes

1 English cucumber, peeled

1 large purple onion (375 g),
peeled and quartered

½ cup (60 g) pickled peppers (pepperoncini)

2 scallions (40 g), trimmed and sliced thinly

edible flowers, such as chive blossoms,
garlic flower, or pansies

White Wine Vinegar and Mustard Dressing
(*see page 87*)

INSTRUCTIONS

For the Croutons

1. Preheat the oven to 400°F.

2. Tear the rye bread into bite-sized pieces, or cube into 1-inch (2.5 cm) cubes, and place in a large mixing bowl. Add the salt, pepper, Parmigiano-Reggiano, and dried spices to the bowl.

3. Drizzle the bread with the 2 tablespoons of olive oil and mix well to coat the pieces.

4. Spread the bread cubes evenly on the baking sheet and place in the oven for 5–10 minutes, or until toasted and slightly browned.

5. Reserve.

For the Steak and Grilled Purple Onion

6. Pat dry your steak and season with kosher salt and black pepper on both sides.

7. Cook to desired temperature. Rest 5–10 minutes before slicing into ½-inch (1 cm) slices.

8. Drizzle your quartered purple onion with extra-virgin olive oil to coat. Place on the grill and cook until soft and slightly charred, about 8 minutes, turning partway through to grill all sides.

To Assemble

9. Wash and dry your butter lettuce and tear into bite-sized pieces. Arrange evenly on a large platter.

10. Wash and halve the cherry tomatoes and arrange them over the lettuce. Slice the peeled cucumber in half lengthwise, then into ¼-inch (0.5 cm) pieces. Layer on top of the tomatoes.

11. Sprinkle the sliced scallions on top and add the pickled peppers around the platter.

12. Add your grilled purple onions.

13. Slice the steak and place on top of your vegetables in a fanlike pattern.

14. Add the croutons and drizzle the whole salad with the vinaigrette.

15. Garnish with pansies and chive flowers.

WHITE WINE VINEGAR AND MUSTARD DRESSING

A tangy light dressing for any fresh salad.

• Makes about ¼ cup •

INGREDIENTS

1½ tablespoons (23 ml) white wine vinegar

1½ tablespoons (23 ml) extra virgin olive oil

1½ tablespoons (23 g) whole-grain mustard

1 teaspoon (7 g) honey

1 pinch of kosher salt

1 head of chive blossoms (optional)

INSTRUCTIONS

1. Add all the ingredients to a small mixing bowl.

2. Tear the chive flowers from the stem and add to the bowl.

3. Whisk to combine.

4. Store in the refrigerator in an airtight glass jar, for up to 5 days.

LOADED OATMEAL COOKIE ICE CREAM SANDWICHES

• Makes 16 large cookies (8 sandwiches) •

This delicious cookie recipe is filled with rolled oats, raisins, chocolate, and dried cranberries. I love serving these as a yummy afterschool snack on most days, but two cookies together with your favorite ice cream makes a creamy Father's Day treat!

INGREDIENTS

2 sticks (230 g) salted butter—slightly softened,
but still cool to the touch

1¼ cups (225 g) light brown sugar (packed)

2 large eggs (about 110 g)

1½ teaspoons vanilla extract

½ teaspoon (1.5 g) kosher salt

1 teaspoon (2.5 g) ground cinnamon

1¾ cups (225 g) all-purpose flour

1 teaspoon (4.3 g) baking powder

3 cups (240 g) old-fashioned rolled oats

1 cup (160 g) raisins or dried cranberries

¾ cup (125 g) white chocolate chips

⅓ cup (55 g) dark chocolate chips

vanilla ice cream

INSTRUCTIONS

1. Preheat the oven to 350°F and line 2 cookie sheets with parchment paper.

2. In the bowl of a stand mixer (or in a large mixing bowl with a hand mixer), cream together the butter and light brown sugar until fluffy.

3. Add the vanilla extract and 2 eggs to the bowl. Beat on medium speed until well combined.

4. In a separate large bowl, combine the flour, salt, baking powder, and ground cinnamon. Fork-stir, then add these ingredients slowly to the creamed butter and sugar, on low to medium speed, until fully blended.

5. Lower the mixer speed and stir in the oatmeal, dried fruit, and chocolate chips until incorporated.

6. Scrape down the bowl and beaters with a rubber spatula, cover the cookie dough, and chill in the refrigerator for at least 15 minutes. This step is important to get the butter to the correct temperature before baking.

7. After chilling, pull out your prepared cookie sheets and measure out 2 tablespoons of dough per cookie. Roll slightly in your hands and place on the cookie sheet. Next, using either the bottom of a drinking glass or a cookie stamp, gently press down evenly on each cookie. We want the cookie dough to flatten and spread slightly. You should be able to fit 6–8 cookies per sheet.

8. Bake in the oven, using the center racks for 13–15 minutes, or until the cookies set with slightly browned edges.

9. Let the cookies cool on the cookie sheets for 5 minutes before transferring to a larger cooling rack. Repeat for each batch.

10. Store in an airtight container until use, and serve by placing a generous scoop of your favorite vanilla ice cream between two cookies for a fantastic dessert sandwich!

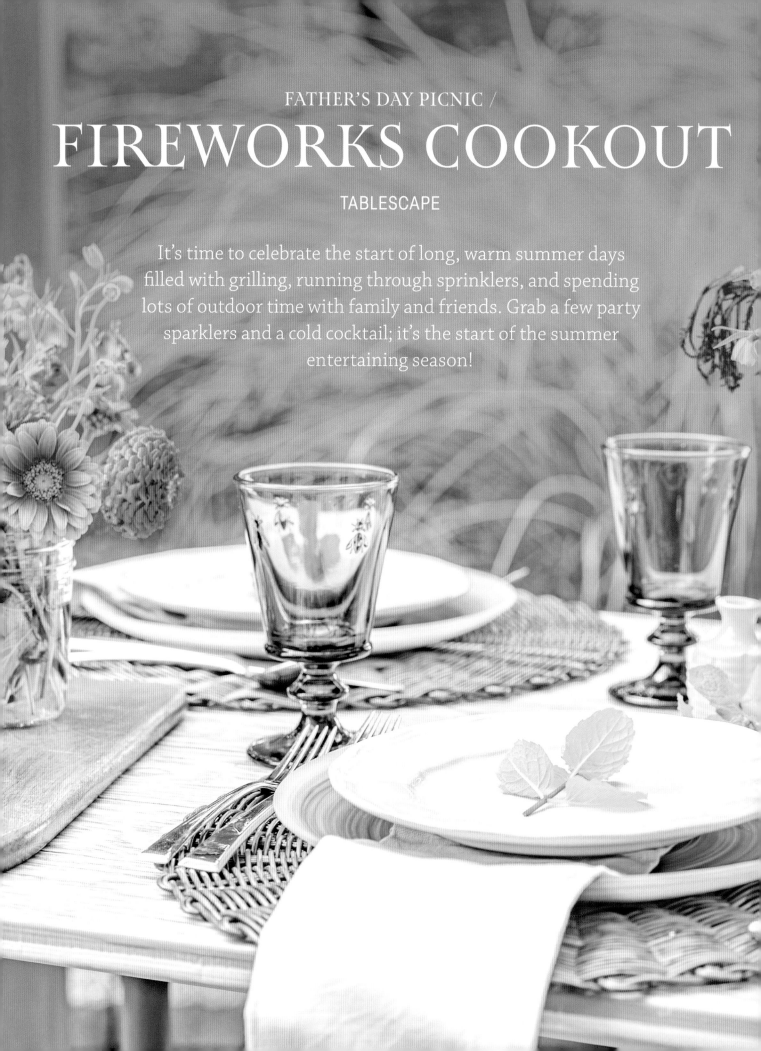

FATHER'S DAY PICNIC /

FIREWORKS COOKOUT

TABLESCAPE

It's time to celebrate the start of long, warm summer days filled with grilling, running through sprinklers, and spending lots of outdoor time with family and friends. Grab a few party sparklers and a cold cocktail; it's the start of the summer entertaining season!

COLOR

I gathered an analogous color palette of vibrant summer shades. Neon pink joins bright orange; magenta and purple flowers play with golden yellows with touches of green. Blue accents help anchor the scene as the firecracker florals brighten the table.

BLOOMS

Multicolored zinnias, golden spider mums, orange gerbera Daisies, and purple larkspur create a classic summer arrangement. I've accented bouquets with magenta Amaranthus stems, to give it that "firecracker" feel!

THE DETAILS

Woven wicker place mats help highlight the blue-glass dinner plates that I've paired with a French country-style ivory salad plate. A mix of Old World tradition with New World whimsy! I'm always a fan of cloth napkins, and these are extra-special ones that have been dip-dyed a bright teal on the bottom edges. Bright blue glasses dot the table, between multiple summer floral arrangements.

WHAT YOU'LL NEED

assorted flowers and 2–3 country-chic vases

woven dark-colored place mats

blue or other colored dinner plates

ivory salad plates

*linen or cotton napkins with a touch of
    complementary color*

lemons

fresh mint sprigs

Set the Table

Location

A porch, patio, or lawn.

Order of Operations

I've set each table setting with a place mat, dinner plate, and salad plate. The napkins are folded into rectangles and slipped under the salad plate about a quarter of the way in, letting the napkin drape off the front edge. Add drinking glasses and silverware. Here I have two flower arrangements just off-center and used leftover flowers to add color to the far ends of the table. I've added a fresh feel to the tablescape by filling any blank spots with fresh lemons and bundles of mint, as well as a small cutting board of sliced lemons.

Small Touches

I've added a pop of color to each setting by placing a sprig of mint on every salad plate. Rather than set pitchers of water on the table, I've saved space by setting up a beverage station just to the side with a large glass dispenser of ice water with lemon and mint.

FIREWORKS COOKOUT

CUCUMBER JALAPEÑO MARGARITA

Spicy, cool, and refreshing, this añejo tequila-based margarita is a crowd favorite. Better yet, it makes as good of a batch drink as it does a single serving!

MY FAVORITE HAMBURGER

One of my childhood memories! These juicy all-beef patties are seasoned with a blend of pantry-staple spices. For me, it's not a cookout without one of these in my hand!

SAUTEED BOK CHOI WITH ROASTED BEETS AND GOAT CHEESE

A lovely warm vegetable side dish, brimming with rich garden flavors and topped with tangy goat cheese. This salad makes me think of summer evenings, and growing things.

CRISPY FRIED EGGPLANT CAPRESE SALAD

Take a traditional caprese salad up a notch! Layers of crispy panko eggplant slices interspersed with fresh tomatoes, mozzarella, and basil. This recipe is a must-try.

RED, WHITE, AND BLUE MIXED-BERRY SHORTCAKES

If you've ever wanted to learn how to make homemade shortcakes, this recipe is your jam! A classic American dessert, featuring plump summer berries and homemade vanilla whipped cream. The shortcakes can be made the day before if desired, but the berries and whipped cream are best the day of.

CUCUMBER JALAPEÑO MARGARITA

• Makes one 18-ounce cocktail •

A perfect margarita—a spicy jalapeño kick, balanced with a kiss of sweetness and smoothed out with cooling cucumber. This margarita recipe uses añejo tequila, an aged spirit with mild vanilla notes. Distinctly different from a blanco or reposado, añejo tequila brings a mellowness that gives this drink a little extra flair.

Note: The longer this drink sits, the spicier it gets! This is due to the heat releasing additional capsaicin oil in the jalapeño. If you're making this as a batch cocktail, I would consider straining the jalapeño rounds out after the initial preparation, unless you enjoy that extra heat, of course!

INGREDIENTS

2 ounces (60 ml) añejo tequila

2 ounces (60 ml) fresh lime juice

1½ ounces (45 ml) Basic Cocktail Simple Syrup
(*see page 39*)

½ ounce (15 ml) orange liqueur

1 fresh jalapeño pepper (25 g)

1 large cucumber

ice

INSTRUCTIONS

1. Peel the cucumber and slice into ¼-inch (0.5 cm) rounds. Slice the jalapeño (keeping the seeds) into ¼-inch (0.5 cm) rounds.

2. Juice the limes, being careful not to include any of the bitter pith (the white part).

3. In the large cup of a cocktail shaker, combine the simple syrup, 3 slices of cucumber, and 2–3 slices of jalapeño.

4. Using a muddler (or the handle of a wooden spoon), muddle the ingredients into the simple syrup. You want to press and twist the muddler into the cucumber and jalapeño pepper to release the juices and oils.

5. Add the lime juice, orange liqueur, and tequila.

6. Scoop a large handful of ice into your shaker. Close the shaker and vigorously shake for 30 seconds to blend (the shaker should become frosted).

7. Fill a large tumbler with ice and place a small cocktail strainer over the top. Strain the cocktail into the glass, catching any seeds or pulp.

8. Garnish with several thinly cut rounds of cucumber and jalapeño pepper. Enjoy immediately!

MY FAVORITE HAMBURGER

• Makes 8 patties •

This is my go-to hamburger recipe. Simple, tasty, and juicy, this burger makes a great base for all of your favorite toppings. I usually serve them up with classic potato buns, slices of ripe tomato and purple onion, lettuce, pickles, and ketchup.

Substitute an equal portion of *Impossible Plant Based Beef Ground* for the ground beef listed. Leave the egg out entirely and replace the Worcestershire sauce with 2 teaspoons (11 g) of organic aged Japanese soy sauce. The distinct umami flavor from the soy sauce will play nicely with the spices.

INGREDIENTS

1 egg (about 50 g)

1 tablespoon (15 ml) Worcestershire sauce

1 tablespoon (9 g) kosher salt

2 teaspoons (7.5 g) garlic powder

2 teaspoons (1.4 g) dried parsley

1 teaspoon (3.2 g) onion powder

1 teaspoon (3.2 g) smoked paprika

¼ teaspoon (0.4 g) freshly ground pepper

40 ounces (1,130 g) 85% lean ground beef

To serve:

hamburger buns; assorted condiments

INSTRUCTIONS

1. In a large mixing bowl, combine the spices, salt, and Worcestershire sauce. Add the egg and lightly beat with a fork to combine.

2. Next, add the ground beef and mix thoroughly by hand (I like to wear disposable gloves to handle the raw meat at this step!).

3. Using a kitchen scale, measure out about 5 ounces (140 g) of the ground-beef mixture and form it into a loose ball (roughly a handful). Flatten into the desired size for your hamburger buns (slightly larger than the bun, since it will shrink slightly) and make a small indent with your thumb, directly in the middle. This helps the burger maintain its shape while cooking. Place the burgers on a large plate, or on a wax-paper-lined cutting board.

4. Repeat this process until you have 8 patties.

5. Grill to your desired temperature, place in a toasted bun, and top with your favorite burger fixings! The seasoned meat will bring every topping to the next level!

SAUTEED BOK CHOI
· Serves 6 ·
WITH ROASTED BEETS AND GOAT CHEESE

Delicious, crunchy, and shaped like an endive with a punk haircut, bok choi is a member of the brassica family of greens. Harvested while still young and more tender, baby bok choi are perfect when quartered and sauteed in butter and olive oil. Here, they join garlic, shallots, and sweet cooked baby beets and are topped with dollops of creamy goat cheese, giving a medley of flavors and textures!

INGREDIENTS

5–6 baby bok choi (650 g total)

6 red baby beets, roasted (250 g) (stores sometimes sell these
cooked and chilled, or you can roast your own)

1 tablespoon (14 g) unsalted butter

1 tablespoon (15 ml) extra-virgin olive oil

1 large clove (5 g) garlic, pressed

1 large shallot (80 g), sliced thinly

2 tablespoons (40 g) plain soft goat cheese

kosher salt

black ground pepper

INSTRUCTIONS

1. Fill a large bowl with cold water and add the baby bok choi.
   Let sit for a few minutes and then agitate. We want to rinse
   out any dirt or grit. Strain and dry.

2. Cut your cooked baby beets into wedges (sixths) and reserve
   (if you don't have precooked baby beets, they can be roasted
   by placing them in the oven for 1 hour at 400°F).

3. Place a large sauté pan over medium-high heat. Add the
   butter and olive oil and heat until foamy.

4. Add the shallots and garlic, then cook until fragrant, about
   3 minutes. Sauté the dried bok choi for 2 minutes. The bok
   choi will turn a bright green as it cooks.

5. Add the beets and stir. Season with a generous pinch of
   kosher salt and fresh black pepper. Cover the pan and let
   cook for about 5 minutes.

6. Uncover and sauté for another 3 minutes to evaporate any
   cooking liquid. Once the bok choi is tender, remove the pan
   from the heat.

7. Using a serving platter or large bowl, pour the vegetables in
   and top with the goat cheese.

CRISPY FRIED EGGPLANT CAPRESE SALAD

• Serves 6–8 •

This is a stunner of a side dish, with crispy panko-breaded slices of eggplant interleaved between fresh, ripe tomatoes, fragrant basil, and creamy mozzarella! To keep this preparation from feeling too "heavy," instead of deep-frying, the dredged eggplant slices are baked at a high temperature with a bit of avocado oil.

INGREDIENTS

1 large eggplant (500 g)

⅓ cup (80 ml) refined avocado oil

3 tablespoons (21 g) all-purpose flour

2 eggs (about 110 g)

1 tablespoon (15 ml) water

½ cup (30 g) plain panko breadcrumbs

1 tablespoon (11 g) garlic powder

2 teaspoons (1.4 g) dried oregano

1 teaspoon (0.7 g) dried parsley

¾ teaspoon (2.5 g) smoked paprika

¾ teaspoon (1.9 g) chili flakes

2 teaspoons (6 g) kosher salt

¼ teaspoon (0.4 g) black pepper

2 tablespoons (10 g) finely grated
Parmigiano-Reggiano cheese

1 ball (16 ounces, or 454 g) buffalo mozzarella

2 large (500 g) ripe tomatoes

1 large handful (10 g) fresh basil leaves

2 sprigs fresh oregano (optional)

aged balsamic vinegar

extra-virgin olive oil

for garnish:
oregano flowers or Italian basil flowers

INSTRUCTIONS

1. Preheat the oven to 425°F.

2. Wash and dry your eggplant. Slice into ¼-inch (0.5 cm) rounds.

3. Place the eggplant rounds on a paper-towel-covered board and lightly sprinkle with kosher salt on both sides. Place another layer of paper towels on top, followed by a wooden cutting board (or some other heavy thing you can use to "squeeze" the moisture out of the eggplant). Let sit for 10–15 minutes. This acts to slightly dry the eggplant before dredging.

4. Once the oven is at temperature, add ⅓ cup of refined avocado oil to a baking tray and place in the hot oven. Allow to heat for about 5–8 minutes. This type of oil is ideal for hot oven use because its smoke point is extremely high.

5. Prepare three shallow bowls for dredging: Add flour to the first bowl. Add two eggs, fork-scrambled, plus 1 tablespoon of water to the second bowl. Add the panko mixed with the dried herbs, grated Parmigiano Reggiano cheese, salt, and pepper to the third bowl.

6. Uncover the eggplant rounds and lightly brush the extra salt off each round with a paper towel.

7. We will now dredge the eggplant and place the coated rounds on a tray. I like to do this assembly-line style, with my left hand doing the flouring only, while my right hand coats the eggplant with egg and Panko. However you prefer to do it, coat the eggplant with flour on both sides and then move the eggplant and coat with egg in the next bowl (allow the egg to drip off the eggplant slightly). Coat with the seasoned panko crumbs in the third bowl and, finally, move to your holding area.

8. Once you have 6–8 eggplant rounds breaded, remove the hot baking tray from the oven and place on a trivet. The tray is now VERY hot, so be careful.

9. Gently transfer the breaded eggplant to the hot oiled tray. It should sizzle on contact!

10. After placing all the rounds, bake in the oven for 10–12 minutes. Flip with tongs and allow to bake another 8 minutes until golden brown. It's fine to work in batches as well.

11. While the eggplant is baking, slice your tomatoes and mozzarella into ¼-inch-thick (0.5 cm) rounds. Wash your herbs and pat dry.

12. When the eggplant is golden brown and crispy on both sides, take the baking sheet out of the oven and transfer onto a paper-toweled plate to drain excess oil.

To Assemble

1. Using a large plate or small platter, arrange the eggplant, tomatoes, hand-torn basil and oregano, and mozzarella in layers. Get creative—there isn't a wrong way to assemble this dish.

2. Sprinkle with salt and fresh pepper. Drizzle the salad with good olive oil and syrupy aged balsamic vinegar to finish.

3. You can garnish with fresh oregano flowers or Italian basil flowers.

RED, WHITE, AND BLUE MIXED-BERRY SHORTCAKES

• Serves 6–8 •

This is a family recipe for strawberry shortcake. I grew up gobbling these delicious shortcakes during summers spent with my cousins on Cape Cod. New England–style shortcakes are as buttery as their southern-style cousins but are less a biscuit and more crumbly like a shortbread cookie. I've refreshed this classic dessert by adding fresh lemon zest to the shortcake dough, along with bright blueberries, lemon-scented geranium flowers, and a big old dollop of vanilla whipped cream.

INGREDIENTS

For the Shortcakes

2 cups (256 g) all-purpose flour

1 tablespoon (13 g) baking powder

¼ teaspoon (0.75 g) salt

½ cup (230 g) salted butter, cold and cubed

½ cup (120 ml) milk

1 tablespoon (10 g) fresh lemon zest

2 tablespoons (26 g) white sugar

2 tablespoons (24 g) turbinado sugar for the tops of the shortcakes

1 teaspoon (4.8 g) vanilla extract

1 egg (about 55 g)

For the Glaze

1 egg yolk + 1 tablespoon (15 ml) half-and-half

For the Berries

1 quart (650 g) fresh strawberries

101

1 pint (340 g) fresh blueberries

2 tablespoons (26 g) white sugar

For the Vanilla Whipped Cream

1 pint (473 ml) heavy whipping cream

2 tablespoons (26 g) white sugar

1 teaspoon (4.8 g) vanilla extract

for garnish:
edible lemon-scented geranium flowers

INSTRUCTIONS

For the Shortcakes

1. Preheat the oven to 450°F and line a baking sheet with parchment paper.

2. In a large bowl, mix together the flour, 2 tablespoons of white sugar, 1 tablespoon of lemon zest, salt, and baking powder.

3. Cut the cold butter into the flour mixture with a pastry cutter (you can do this in a food processor as well, but I prefer to do it by hand). Keep "cutting" the butter into the flour until the whole mixture looks like coarse crumbs.

4. In a small bowl, lightly beat the whole egg.

5. Add the milk, egg, and vanilla extract to the bowl with the dry ingredients. Stir together until everything is moistened. You don't want to overmix the dough (that makes for tough shortcakes), so just get the ingredients incorporated. There will be some flour pockets left, which is fine for this type of baking.

6. Transfer the dough onto a well-floured surface and kneed for 8–10 pushes—just enough to barely bring the shortcake dough together. Shape and flatten the dough into a circle about ¾ inch thick.

7. Using a lightly floured biscuit cutter or 3-inch-diameter drinking glass, cut out several circles and transfer to the lined baking sheet. You want to have 6–7 rounds. After completing the first batch, gently bring the dough together and flatten again, to cut batch #2.

8. Once the shortcakes have been cut and transferred to the baking sheet, take a small bowl and fork-whisk the egg yolk and half-and-half to make the glaze. Brush the tops of the shortcakes with the glaze and sprinkle the tops with turbinado sugar (or raw sugar).

9. Bake for 12–15 minutes, or until perfectly golden.

10. Transfer to a wire rack to cool.

For the Berries

1. Wash and dry all the berries.

2. Trim the tops off the strawberries and slice into thin ⅛-inch (0.25 cm) slices. Add the strawberries to a medium-sized bowl along with the blueberries.

3. Sprinkle the berries with 2 tablespoons white sugar and toss gently. Set aside to macerate.

For the Vanilla Whipped Cream

1. Place your stand mixing bowl and whisk attachment into the freezer for 10 minutes, to chill the equipment. This will help you whip up the cream.

2. After chilling, pour the pint of cold whipping cream into the mixing bowl and beat on low for 30 seconds, using the wire attachment. Raise to medium-high speed for 1–2 minutes, or until the mix starts to thicken.

3. Turn off the mixer and add the sugar and vanilla extract, then restart the mixer on medium-high speed, beating until thickened and fluffy, usually another 2–4 minutes.

4. Be careful to not overbeat! The mix will become sweet butter instead of fluffy whipped cream!

To Assemble

1. Cut one of the cooled shortcakes in half, horizontally. Place a spoonful of berries and juices on top of the shortcake and then a generous layer of whipped cream. Place the other shortcake half on top of the whipped cream and add a few extra berries and whipped cream over everything.

2. Garnish with lemon-scented geranium flowers.

SUMMER SOLSTICE GARDEN PARTY

SOLSTICE BASIL SMASH

A refreshing and herbaceous summer gin cocktail, this is the perfect welcome drink for your guests as they arrive to celebrate the summer solstice.

FRESH BURRATA CHEESE WITH HONEYED NECTARINES AND MELON

An elegant burrata salad recipe, filled with fresh stone fruit, melons, and basil.

SEARED AHI TUNA WITH LIME AND HERB GREMOLATA, GREEN GRAPES, AND A HONEY-LIME VINAIGRETTE

Beautiful and easy to make, this stunning tuna appetizer is full of fresh garden flavors. The vinaigrette can be made up to a day in advance.

CREAMY TRUFFLE AND SHIITAKE MUSHROOM PAPPARDELLE

Pappardelle pasta is pan-tossed with a creamy sauce of sauteed shiitake mushrooms, shallot, fragrant truffle butter, and garlic. Garnished with basil blossoms.

APRICOT GALETTE WITH ELDERFLOWER WHIPPED CREAM

Bright and floral, this apricot galette combines fresh and dried fruits. I've elevated the intense apricot flavors with elderflower liqueur in both the filling and the whipped topping.

SOLSTICE BASIL SMASH

• Makes one 8-ounce cocktail •

Loaded with fresh citrus and fragrant green basil, which is the perfect counterpoint to the floral notes of the gin.

INGREDIENTS

2 ounces (60 ml) freshly squeezed pink grapefruit juice

1 ounce (30 ml) freshly squeezed lemon juice

2 ounces (60 ml) floral-style gin, such as
The Botanist or Monkey 47

1.5 ounces (45 ml) Basic Cocktail Simple Syrup
(*see page 39*)

1 handful (10 g) fresh green basil

ice

for garnish:
pink grapefruit rounds, a grapefruit twist, fresh basil,
or edible blooms like dianthus and alyssum flowers

INSTRUCTIONS

1. Start by adding the lemon juice to the large cup of a cocktail shaker.

2. Gently "smack" the fresh basil on the back of your palm and add to the shaker as well.

3. Using a muddler, gently twist the basil to express the oils.

4. Add the pink grapefruit juice, simple syrup, and floral gin; fill half of the shaker with ice; and close.

5. Briskly shake your cocktail for 30 seconds, or until the shaker becomes frosted over.

6. Fill a double Old-Fashioned glass with ice, then strain the drink into the glass with a Hawthorne strainer.

7. Garnish with grapefruit, herbs, or flowers.

FRESH BURRATA CHEESE
WITH HONEYED NECTARINES AND MELON

Is there anything better than a creamy summer burrata salad? Fresh tomatoes, nectarines, ripe melon, and garden herbs join to make this fresh Italian cheese sing!

INGREDIENTS

For the Salad

2 slices fresh watermelon, sliced on the thicker side (½ inch, or 1 cm thick)

2 slices fresh cantaloupe, sliced on the thinner side (¼ inch, or 0.5 cm thick)

¼ cup (48 g) pitted cherries

½ cup (80 g) fresh strawberries

1 medium (250 g) tomato, cut into eighths

1 handful (10 g) fresh basil leaves

6 fresh mint leaves

2 sprigs lemon thyme, optional

4 ounces (115 g) fresh burrata cheese, ball

for garnish:
edible flowers such as pansies, thyme blossoms, and nasturtium blossoms and leaves

For the Honeyed Nectarines

2 large nectarines

1 tablespoon (30 ml) extra-virgin olive oil

½ lime, juiced (15 ml juice)

1 teaspoon (7 g) honey

pinch of salt

4 fresh mint leaves

2 sprigs lemon thyme, optional

For the Shallot and Champagne Vinegar Dressing

½ large shallot (40 g) sliced into thin rings

¼ cup (60 ml) champagne vinegar

pinch kosher salt

¼ cup (60 ml) extra-virgin olive oil

2 teaspoons (14 g) honey

¼ clove garlic (1.5 g), smashed and minced

pinch of black pepper

INSTRUCTIONS

For the Salad

1. Cube the watermelon slices and trim the cantaloupe slices into thin triangles. Set aside.

2. Halve the fresh cherries and place in a small bowl. Destem and halve the strawberries, then place in a small bowl until use.

3. Stem the tomato and cut into eighths. Set aside.

4. Wash and dry your herbs.

For the Honeyed Nectarines

1. Pit and thinly slice the nectarines. Add to a small mixing bowl.

2. Next, add the olive oil, lime juice, honey, and salt.

3. Roughly tear the fresh mint and add to the bowl. Add the leaves of two sprigs of lemon thyme (optional).

4. Mix to combine.

For the Dressing

1. In a medium glass jar with lid, add the champagne vinegar, salt, and shallot slices. Let sit for 5 minutes.

2. Add the olive oil, honey, garlic, and black pepper.

3. Close the jar with a tightly fitted lid and shake vigorously. Let sit in the refrigerator until use.

To Assemble

1. Reserve a large, shallow bowl or small platter.

2. Place the fresh burrata ball into the center of the large shallow bowl.

3. Start to arrange the watermelon cubes and cantaloupe slices around the burrata.

4. Add the cherries, tomatoes, and strawberries on top of the melon and where you think the dish could use more color.

5. Place hand-torn fresh basil, mint, and lemon thyme throughout.

6. Dress with the champagne vinegar dressing and garnish with edible flowers and herbs.

SEARED AHI TUNA

• Serves 6–8 •

WITH LIME AND HERB GREMOLATA, GREEN GRAPES, AND A HONEY-LIME VINAIGRETTE

Impress your guests with this gorgeous summer ahi tuna appetizer! Using good-quality tuna loin, we'll quickly sear the fish, then layer it with bright citrus, fresh herbs, and juicy green grapes.

INGREDIENTS

For the Vinaigrette

3 tablespoons (45 ml) extra-virgin olive oil

2 tablespoons (30 ml) fresh lime juice

½ tablespoon (11 g) honey

For the Lime and Herb Gremolata

¼ cup (5 g) packed fresh cilantro

3 tablespoons (15 g) minced fresh chives

½ teaspoon (1.5 g) freshly grated lime zest

1 teaspoon (5 ml) extra-virgin olive oil

Pinch of kosher salt and black ground pepper

For the Ahi Tuna

8 ounces (230 g) ahi tuna loin

1 (25 g) fresh jalapeño pepper

⅓ cup (50 g) green grapes

1 fresh pink grapefruit

¼ cup (38 g) yellow or orange grape tomatoes

for garnish:
edible flowers such as marigolds, pansies,
and purple basil blossoms

INSTRUCTIONS

For the Vinaigrette

Add the oil, lime juice, and honey to a small mixing bowl and whisk to combine.

For the Lime and Herb Gremolata

1. Remove the cilantro leaves from the stems. Roughly chop the cilantro and add to a small mixing bowl, along with the fresh chives and lime zest.

2. Sprinkle in the salt and pepper and add the olive oil. Mix to combine.

For the Ahi Tuna

1. Pat dry the ahi tuna loin and lightly season with salt.

2. Quickly sear in a hot cast-iron skillet or plancha. We are just touching all the sides of the ahi tuna to the heat for ten seconds or so, to create a slight sear. Let rest.

To Assemble

1. Cut the jalapeño into the thinnest rounds you possibly can. Reserve in ice water.

2. Slice the green grapes and tomatoes into thin rounds as well (these do not have to be as thin as the jalapeño).

3. Slice the ahi tuna into ¼-inch (0.5 cm) pieces with a very sharp knife.

4. Lay the slices on a medium-sized platter at different angles, but with equal space between them.

5. Dollop each slice with a bit of the herb gremolata.

6. Add the thin slices of jalapeño pepper, grapes, and tomato to the sliced tuna. Scatter some of the rounds between the slices as well.

7. Peel the pink grapefruit and slice open one of the segments to expose the small citrus kernels (juice sacs). Pull apart several of these little juice sacs at a time and use them to garnish the tuna.

8. Drizzle the honey-lime vinaigrette over the tuna and platter.

9. Garnish with edible flowers.

CREAMY TRUFFLE AND SHIITAKE MUSHROOM PAPPARDELLE

• Serves 6 •

Pappardelle pasta is tossed with a decadent sauce of truffle butter, shiitake mushrooms, Parmigiano Reggiano cheese, and a splash of cream. Topped with fresh green basil and white basil flowers, this is a luxurious dish for any supper!

Note: This recipe uses a dried pappardelle to attain a more toothsome texture than can be achieved with fresh pasta. Look for pappardelle with a rough, raspy appearance (which is usually due to its being extruded through a bronze die), because it will hold the sauce better than a smooth noodle.

INGREDIENTS

10 ounces (280 g) dried pappardelle pasta

4–5 quarts of water

kosher salt

1 tablespoon (14 g) unsalted butter

1 tablespoon (15 ml) extra-virgin olive oil

2 tablespoons (20 g) minced shallots

¼ cup (30 g) finely diced yellow onion

6 ounces (170 g) shiitake mushrooms, sliced thinly

2 cloves (10 g) fresh garlic, pressed

2 tablespoons (28 g) truffle butter (or substitute 1
teaspoon [5 ml] truffle oil)

½ cup (40 g) finely grated Parmigiano-Reggiano cheese

2 tablespoons (30 ml) heavy cream

¾ cup (340 g) reserved pasta water

¼ teaspoon (0.8 g) lemon zest

hot pepper flakes (optional)

INSTRUCTIONS

1. In a large pasta pot, bring 4 quarts (4,000 ml) of water to a boil, with a large pinch of salt.

2. While waiting for the pasta water to boil, take a large skillet over medium heat with 1 tablespoon of unsalted butter and 1 tablespoon of extra-virgin olive oil. Heat until the butter is foaming.

3. Add the minced shallot and diced onion to the pan, plus a pinch of salt and pepper. Cook for 4 minutes, while stirring occasionally.

4. Next, add the sliced mushrooms and cook down, about 5 minutes.

5. Add the garlic and cook for 2 additional minutes, while stirring occasionally. Add the truffle butter or truffle oil to the pan.

6. The pasta water should now be at a boil; add pappardelle and let cook for 9 minutes (or as directed for al dente) uncovered, while stirring occasionally.

7. After the pasta is cooked to al dente, ladle out about ¾ cup of pasta water into the sauce and drain the remaining water.

8. Add the grated Parmigiano-Reggiano and heavy cream to the sauce and bring to a simmer, stirring to incorporate all ingredients. Adjust the salt and pepper to taste.

9. Add the drained pappardelle to the sauce and toss to coat. Let cook an additional 1 minute with everything together in the skillet.

10. Transfer the pasta to a serving bowl. Garnish with more grated Parmigiano Reggiano, fresh lemon zest, fresh green

APRICOT GALETTE

WITH ELDERFLOWER WHIPPED CREAM

This dreamy apricot galette with sourdough butter crust is topped with a pillowy elderflower whipped cream. If you don't have any sourdough scrap around, no stress—just use a traditional butter crust recipe. Pretty as a flower garden, and baked in an hour, this is a lovely way to celebrate the summer solstice!

INGREDIENTS

For the Crust

2⅔ cups (340 g) all-purpose flour

1 tablespoon (13 g) sugar

1 pinch (1.2 g) salt

1 cup (230 g) cold butter, cut into chunks

¼ cup (25 g) sourdough starter scrap

2 tablespoons (30 ml) cold water

For the Apricot Filling

½ cup (100 g) + 4 tablespoons (50 g) sugar, divided

¼ cup (60 ml) elderflower liqueur

1 cup (120 g) dried apricots, sliced into strips

6 fresh apricots (210 g total), washed and pitted

¼ cup (60 ml) water

3 tablespoons (21 g) cornstarch

1 teaspoon (5 ml) fresh lemon juice

2 tablespoons (16 g) all-purpose flour

2 tablespoons (14 g) almond flour

pinch of kosher salt (1.2 g)

1 egg (about 55 g)

1 tablespoon (15 ml) milk

raw sugar for sprinkling

For the Elderflower Whipped Cream

½ cup (120 ml) heavy cream, cold

1½ tablespoons (23 ml) elderflower liqueur

1½ tablespoons (20 g) sugar

for garnish:
fresh lavender blossoms

INSTRUCTIONS

For the Crust

1. In the bowl of a food processor, add the flour, salt, and sugar. Pulse several times to mix.

2. Begin adding the chunks of butter to the flour mix, pulsing between additions. Try to incorporate each chunk separately until you get a sandy texture.

3. Scoop in the ¼ cup of sourdough starter scrap and drizzle in the cold water while mixing in several long pulses. Blend the dough until it just barely comes together.

4. Transfer the dough to a floured board and work it into a rough ball. Split the dough into 2 portions with a sharp knife, then shape each into a disc. Wrap tightly in plastic wrap and let chill in the fridge for 1 hour. You can freeze the extra dough or make another galette with the second portion!

To Make the Apricot Filling

1. In a small saucepan, bring 4 tablespoons (50 g) of sugar, ¼ cup (60 ml) of elderflower liqueur, and ¼ cup (60 ml) of water to a boil, while whisking occasionally. Let boil for 2 minutes and then place off the heat. This is your sugar syrup.

2. While the syrup is heating, cut the dried apricots into strips and place into a heatproof bowl. Once the syrup is finished boiling, carefully pour the syrup over the dried apricots to rehydrate them slightly and let them cool.

3. Pit your fresh apricots and slice thinly (about ¼ inch, or 0.5 cm). Add to a medium-sized bowl.

4. Strain the rehydrated apricots from the syrup (saving the syrup for brushing on the finished galette) and mix all the apricots together with 1 teaspoon (5 ml) of fresh lemon juice, 3 tablespoons (21 g) of cornstarch, and ½ cup (100 g) of sugar. Stir well to combine.

To Assemble

1. Preheat the oven to 400°F.

2. Place a piece of parchment paper on your work surface and flour lightly.

3. Flour a rolling pin and roll out the pie dough into a rough circle, about ⅛ inch thick.

4. In a small bowl, mix 2 tablespoons (25 g) of sugar, 2 tablespoons (16 g) of flour, 2 tablespoons (14 g) of almond flour, and a pinch of salt. Spread this mixture into the center of the dough and pat down to spread out slightly.

5. Add the apricot filling on top of the mixture and spread, leaving about 2 inches (5 cm) of the pie dough bare as a border (this will be folded over).

6. Begin to fold sections of the pie dough edges toward the center, slightly overlapping as you go. Be careful not to tear the dough near the bottom, since you'll spring a leak, and all of your delicious juices will escape! Gently press and pinch as you fold the edges to keep the shape.

7. Whisk 1 egg with a splash of milk in a bowl. Brush onto the pie dough with a pastry brush to help seal any small leaks and create a lovely, glossy baked crust. Sprinkle the pie dough with raw sugar to finish.

8. Transfer the galette, on the parchment paper, to a baking sheet.

9. Bake for 1 hour or until the center is bubbling.

10. Let cool to room temperature before serving.

11. Optionally, boil the leftover sugar syrup on medium-high heat until reduced by half. Remove from the heat and brush the syrup over the exposed fruit filling of the cooled galette.

For the Elderflower Whipped Cream

1. Place the heavy cream into a large bowl and begin to whisk vigorously. You can do this by hand, or with a stand mixer.

2. Once the cream begins to show soft peaks, add the sugar and elderflower liqueur.

3. Continue to whisk until you get fluffy, high peaks.

4. Serve on top of the galette.

5. Garnish with fresh, food-grade lavender flowers.

GARDEN PARTY

TABLESCAPE

There's something very magical about the summer solstice. It celebrates the longest day of the year and the picturesque image that summer conjures up, of gardens overflowing with scented flowers, warm evenings filled with fireflies, and walking barefoot in the cool grass. Gather your closest friends and enjoy a table full of succulent fruits, colorful flourishes, and lush details.

COLOR

I wanted to evoke a fairylike feeling to this summer tablescape! An analogous palate of bright reds, hot pink, apricots, and lush greens infuse our floral arrangements. Touches of white and yellow, and blue and orange, give the table a feeling of extravagance.

BLOOMS

large red garden roses, apricot roses, echinacea, chamomile, flowers, spray roses, and ruffle-like ranunculus are arranged with a variety of greenery, including ferns, Queen Anne's lace, goldenrod, and wild vines

THE DETAILS

Several pairs of glass and crystal candlesticks with long tapers line the table. I wanted to emphasize bright color and juicy fruits, so I incorporated bowls of ripe berries and wedges of chilled melons across the table. Neutral-colored dishware with textural details helps highlight the light-pink cheesecloth napkins and nature-inspired napkin rings. I wanted this table to be worthy of a midsummer night's dream!

WHAT YOU'LL NEED

1 large vase + 1 medium vase, preferably or stone or wood

assorted flowers

a white or neutral-colored tablecloth

a burnt-orange or other colorful table runner

an array of glass and crystal candlesticks with tapered candles

organically textured place mats

neutral-colored dishware

brightly colored glassware in blue and yellow

pink napkins or complementary-colored linens

golden napkin rings

small decorative bowls, cake stands, and plates

decorative moss, fruits, and sweets

Set the Table

Location

A shady patio or lawn.

Order of Operations

Begin by spreading out your tablecloth and laying the table runner down the center of the space. Next, add your large floral arrangement to one side of the table, and your medium-sized floral arrangement to the other side. Start to fill in the center of the table with your candlesticks, small bowls and plates of fruits and sweets, small arrangements of flowers with decorative moss, and cake stands filled with cut melon. Set each table setting with a place mat, dinner plate, salad plate, and glass, along with a napkin with napkin ring.

Small Touches

I wanted to stay mindful of our dreamlike theme, so I made sure to reserve several stems of flowers from our arrangements to use on the table itself. I then gathered these blooms together with loose fruits like cherries and grapes, along with decorative mosses to create organic resting spots for our guests' view. Creating little vignettes on your table is a fun and unique way to make your party stand out!

117

STRAWBERRY SEASON BRUNCH

STRAWBERRY RHUBARB SHRUB

A vintage cocktail (or easy mocktail!) with a long food history, and regarded as one of the first thirst quenchers. Made with juicy strawberries and tart rhubarb. The shrub base can be made in advance and refrigerated for weeks to months.

WHIPPED-FETA TOASTS WITH BERRIES AND BEETS

These "fancy toasts" combine tangy feta cheese with Greek yogurt, herbs, roasted beets, strawberries, and honey. A simply gorgeous combination of sweet, salty, and savory. The beets can be roasted up to two days in advance, if needed.

SEARED SALMON SALAD WITH STRAWBERRIES, GOAT CHEESE, AND CANDIED PECANS

This is an easy and elegant way to serve salmon as a main course. Perfectly seared salmon sits on top of baby greens, berries, candied nuts, and goat cheese. Drizzled with a homemade creamy basil yogurt dressing. The pecans can be made up to 3 days in advance, and the basil yogurt can be made the day before, if desired.

SOFT STRAWBERRY ROLLS WITH ELDERFLOWER ICING

Pillowy soft and stuffed with three different preparations of strawberries, every bite is the "perfect bite" when it comes to these pastries.

MINI CHOCOLATE TRIFLES WITH CHAMPAGNE WHIPPED CREAM

This low-fuss dessert will be sure to impress your guests! Layers of rich chocolate cake, homemade berry coulis, and champagne-infused whipped cream create a stunning version of a traditional trifle dessert. The coulis can be made the day before, and the cake can be made up to two days in advance if needed.

STRAWBERRY RHUBARB SHRUB

• Makes two 6-ounce cocktails •

A shrub is an age-old drink base made from sugars, fruit, and acid. Seriously, they were drinking versions of this type of refresher in the colonial era! I use it as a starter for cocktails and zero-proof summer coolers. I've updated a classic shrub with beautiful strawberries and rhubarb, a dash of vodka, and a little bit of elderflower liqueur to jazz it up. Turn the shrub concentrate into a delicious mocktail by substituting club soda for the liqueur.

INGREDIENTS

2 strawberries (50 g) washed and trimmed
(plus more for garnish)

1.5 ounces (45 ml) Rhubarb and Strawberry Shrub Syrup
(*see page 120*)

3 ounces (90 ml) vodka
(I prefer Polish or Swedish varieties)

1 ounce (30 ml) elderflower liqueur

1 ounce (30 ml) club soda

ice

for garnish: edible flowers such as pansies or cosmos

INSTRUCTIONS

1. Reserve two lowball glasses. Take a strawberry and cut about ½ inch into the bottom. Run the cut end of the strawberry around the rim of the glasses (this will lend a beautiful strawberry scent to the glass, since the vinegar acidity of the shrub can be overpowering to some).

2. In a cocktail shaker cup, add 2 halved strawberries and mash with a muddler.

3. Add the shrub syrup, vodka, and elderflower liqueur.

4. Fill the shaker cup with a small handful of ice and shake vigorously until well chilled.

5. Fill your lowball glasses halfway with ice, then strain the cocktail into the glasses. Add a splash of seltzer water and mix gently.

6. Garnish with strawberries, rhubarb ribbons, or edible flowers.

Strawberry Rhubarb Shrub Syrup

Shrubs are a very flexible drink flavor base: they can be enjoyed in cocktails and nonalcoholic drinks alike. Known to be enjoyed since biblical times, this lightly fermented fruit syrup found popularity in the West during the 18th century. Add some to your favorite mixed drink instead of citrus juices, or mix together with soda water and ice for a very light and refreshing beverage.

• Makes 1 cup •

INGREDIENTS

1½ cups (180 g) fresh rhubarb, chopped

½ cup (80 g) fresh strawberries, trimmed and chopped

1 cup (200 g) sugar

1 cup (236 ml) apple cider vinegar
(you can use white vinegar, but it will be more aggressively acidic)

a large glass jar

INSTRUCTIONS

1. Preheat the oven to 350°F and place a piece of parchment paper on the baking sheet.

2. Add the pecans to the baking sheet and roast for about 5–7 minutes, or until fragrant. Nuts can burn easily, so keep an eye on them.

3. Remove the baking sheet from the oven and cool.

4. In a large skillet on medium-high heat, add the brown sugar, water, salt, and spices. Mix well (the sugar will melt quickly).

5. Add the pecans to the melted sugar mixture and stir to coat (keep the baking sheet and paper ready). Let cook for about 5 minutes, while stirring. Lower the heat if you notice that the nuts are cooking too quickly. The coating will become slightly shiny and shouldn't be sticky by the end of the cooking process.

6. Spread the candied nuts on the parchment paper and let cool. Store in an airtight container until use.

WHIPPED-FETA TOASTS
WITH BERRIES AND BEETS • Serves 6 •

With its smooth texture and tangy flavor, this whipped spread makes an amazing base layer for our sweet fruit and fresh herb topping. A delightful summer mixture of fresh cherries, strawberries, and roasted beets help elevate the feta spread and is capped off with a sprinkle of raw pistachios.

INGREDIENTS

8 ounces (225 g) feta cheese

½ cup (112 g) regular (full fat) plain Greek yogurt

¼ cup (60 ml) extra-virgin olive oil + 2 tablespoons (30 ml), divided

4 sprigs fresh dill

4 sprigs fresh lemon thyme
(if not available, substitute 4 sprigs thyme +
¼ teaspoon (0.8 g) lemon zest)

salt and pepper to taste

4 small roasted beets (160 g), peeled

1 cup (160 g) fresh strawberries

⅓ cup (60 g) fresh cherries

¼ (75 g) English cucumber

1 + 1 tablespoons (21 g + 21 g) honey, divided

½ fresh lime, juiced (15 ml juice)

6 fresh mint leaves

¼ cup (38 g) raw pistachios

6 slices crusty sourdough bread

1 tablespoon (15 ml) extra-virgin olive oil

1 tablespoon (14 g) salted butter

for garnish:
edible flowers and herbs such as violets, pansies, and
nasturtium leaves and flowers

4. Take the raw pistachios and place in a large resealable plastic bag. Gently crush with a rolling pin or other heavy item.

To Make the Toasts

1. Preheat the oven to 350°F.

2. Melt 1 tablespoon of salted butter with 1 tablespoon of olive oil and mix together.

3. Using a pastry brush or spoon, spread the olive oil / butter mixture on both sides of 6 pieces of crusty sliced bread. Place on a baking sheet.

4. Bake for 5 minutes, or until golden. Flip the slices and bake once more for 2–3 minutes. Be careful not to burn.

5. Let cool and reserve.

To Assemble a "Make Your Own" Platter:

1. Spread a generous layer of whipped feta on ⅓ of your platter.

2. Spoon the honeyed fruit and vegetable topping next to the whipped feta, right down the middle of the plate.

3. Tear the toasted sourdough into large pieces and add along the final third of the plate.

4. Sprinkle the whipped feta with the crushed pistachios.

5. Garnish the fruit mixture with edible flowers, mint leaves, and fresh dill.

Alternative Plating: Create several premade toasts by spreading the whipped feta on individual toasts and then generously topping with the fruit and herb topping, pistachios, fresh herbs, and edible flowers.

INSTRUCTIONS

To Make the Whipped Feta

1. In the bowl of a food processor, add the feta, Greek yogurt, and olive oil. Blend until smooth. If the mixture seems too thick, you can add a splash more olive oil.

2. Add the leaves of 2 sprigs of lemon thyme, the leaves of two small sprigs of dill, and salt and pepper to taste. Blend briefly to combine, then transfer to a small bowl. Refrigerate.

For the Toppings

1. Pit and halve the cherries. Destem and halve the strawberries. Quarter your roasted small beets (baby beets can be purchased precooked, or you can roast them at 400°F for one hour). Peel the cucumber and dice.

2. Add all the fruits and vegetables to a medium-sized mixing bowl. Add the juice of ½ a fresh lime, 2 tablespoons of honey, and 1 tablespoon of extra-virgin olive oil and mix.

3. Tear the mint leaves and add to the fruits, along with the leaves of 2 sprigs of lemon thyme (or, the leaves of 2 regular sprigs of thyme + ¼ teaspoon of fresh lemon zest). Mix to combine, then salt and pepper to taste.

SEARED SALMON SALAD
WITH STRAWBERRIES, GOAT CHEESE, AND CANDIED PECANS · Serves 6 ·

Salmon is a wonderful light protein for brunch. It is easy to make, and it pairs beautifully with this sweet and tangy salad. Simple layers of fresh greens, strawberries, blueberries, and goat cheese are complemented by homemade candied pecans for crunch.

INGREDIENTS

For the Salad

32 ounces (900 g) fresh center-cut salmon filet

1 tablespoon (15 ml) extra-virgin olive oil

generous pinch of kosher salt

6 cups (180 g) mixed baby greens

2 cups (320 g) fresh strawberries

¼ cup (40 g) fresh blueberries

¼ (90 g) of a purple onion

4 ounces (113 g) creamy plain goat cheese

½ cup (60 g) Candied Pecans (*see page 124*)

For the Dressing

1½ tablespoon (23 ml) extra-virgin olive oil

1 tablespoon (15 ml) fresh lemon juice

¼ teaspoon (0.8 g) fresh lemon zest

½ clove (2.5 g) garlic, minced

½ tablespoon (2.5 g) Dijon mustard

½ tablespoon (11 g) honey

2 chive blossoms, roughly chopped (optional)

for garnish:
chive blossoms, borage blossoms, or dianthus

INSTRUCTIONS

For the Salmon

1. Using several paper towels, pat dry the salmon and trim any skin away.

2. Preheat a cast-iron skillet on high and add 1 tablespoon (15 ml) olive oil.

3. Slice your salmon filet into 6 portions, using a very sharp knife. Season the fish quickly with kosher salt.

4. After the olive oil has started to smoke, place the salmon in the pan. To create a good sear, start with about 5 minutes of cooking time on the top side, then flip over and finish with 1–2 minutes on the bottom side. We are going for crispy tops, with a soft and moist inside, not dry.

For the Dressing

Add the 1½ tablespoons (23 ml) of olive oil, lemon juice, zest, garlic, mustard, and honey to a jam jar with a tightly fitted lit. Close and shake vigorously for 30 seconds. Reserve in the refrigerator.

For the Salad

1. Prepare 6 salad plates.

2. Spread a handful of fresh greens on each plate.

3. Destem and halve the strawberries before adding to each plate evenly.

4. Thinly slice the purple onion, and layer on top of the greens.

5. Add the blueberries and candied pecans to each plate.

6. Place a portion of salmon on each plate, and the desired amount of goat cheese.

7. Drizzle with the dressing and add the edible flowers for garnish.

Candied Pecans

· Makes 1½ cups (180 g) ·

INGREDIENTS

1½ cups (168 g) raw whole pecans

¾ cup (90 g) light brown sugar

2 tablespoons (30 ml) water

1 teaspoon (2.5 g) ground cinnamon

¼ teaspoon (0.7 g) ground (dried) ginger

1 pinch (1.2 g) kosher salt

INSTRUCTIONS

1. Preheat the oven to 350°F and place a piece of parchment paper on the baking sheet.

2. Add the pecans to the baking sheet and roast for about 5–7 minutes, or until fragrant. Nuts can burn easily, so keep an eye on them.

3. Remove the baking sheet from the oven and cool.

4. In a large skillet on medium-high heat, add the brown sugar, water, salt, and spices. Mix well (the sugar will melt quickly).

5. Add the pecans to the melted sugar mixture and stir to coat (keep the baking sheet and paper ready). Let cook for about 5 minutes, while stirring. Lower the heat if you notice that the nuts are cooking too quickly. The coating will become slightly shiny and shouldn't be sticky by the end of the cooking process.

6. Spread the candied nuts on the parchment paper and let cool. Store in an airtight container until use.

SOFT STRAWBERRY ROLLS
WITH ELDERFLOWER ICING · Serves 8 ·

These are the most tender and fluffy sweet rolls that I've ever made! Using a unique Japanese milk bread starter called tangzhong, the dough bakes up extra moist and puffy, due to the dried milk proteins. Instead of rolling it up with cinnamon sugar, we'll fill these delicious rolls with 3 preparations of strawberries: fresh, freeze-dried, and sweet jam. Topped with a floral elderflower icing, this recipe is a strawberry dream!

INGREDIENTS

For the Tangzhong Starter

5 tablespoons (75 ml) water

5 tablespoons (75 ml) whole milk

3 tablespoons + 1 teaspoon (27 g total) all-purpose flour

For the Dough

4 cups (512 g) + 2 tablespoons (16 g) all-purpose flour

¼ cup (50 g) sugar

1¾ teaspoons (5.25 g) kosher salt

1 tablespoon (11 g) instant yeast

¼ cup (23 g) nonfat dry milk powder

¾ cup (175 ml) whole milk, warmed

6 tablespoons (85 g) butter, melted

2 large eggs (about 110 g), at room temperature

Tangzhong Starter (*see above*)

For the Filling

1 cup (160 g) whole fresh strawberries, trimmed and diced

¼ cup (5 g) freeze-dried strawberries, crushed

¼ cup (80 g) strawberry jam

½ cup (100 g) sugar

1 teaspoon (4.8 g) vanilla extract

2 teaspoons (6.5 g) fresh lemon zest

6 tablespoons (85 g) butter, softened (this will be placed between the dough and the strawberry filling)

For the Elderflower Icing

1 cup (225 g) cream cheese

3 tablespoons (42 g) butter, softened

1½ cup (192 g) confectioner's sugar

1 tablespoon (15 ml) fresh lemon juice

2 tablespoons (30 ml) whole milk

1 tablespoon (15 ml) elderflower liqueur

pinch of kosher salt

INSTRUCTIONS

For the Tangzhong Starter

1. In a small saucepan, combine the 5 tablespoons (75 ml) of water, 5 tablespoons (75 ml) of whole milk, and 3 tablespoons + 1 teaspoon (27 g) of flour. Whisk to combine.

2. Place over medium heat and continue whisking until thickened into a paste (about 5 minutes), being careful not to brown the starter. Remove from the heat and reserve.

For the Dough

1. In the bowl of a stand mixer, using a dough hook attachment, combine the additional flour, white sugar, salt, dry milk powder, instant yeast, warmed milk, melted butter and eggs.

2. Add the tangzhong starter to the stand mixer bowl.

3. Mix on medium speed for about 3 minutes, or until a rough dough is formed.

4. Remove any dough sticking to the hook and cover the mixing bowl with a tea towel.

5. Place the bowl somewhere warm and let rest for 25 minutes.

6. After resting, place the bowl and the dough hook back on the stand mixer.

7. On medium-high speed, knead the dough with the dough hook for about 2 minutes, or until the dough is smooth and forms a nice ball.

8. Take a large mixing bowl and lightly grease with vegetable oil. Place the dough ball into the oiled bowl and cover with a tea towel.

9. Let the dough rise for about 60 minutes in a warm environment, until it has doubled in size. (You can test this stage by pressing your finger into the dough ball and seeing if your finger makes a permanent dent. If the dent doesn't fade, you're ready to roll!)

For the Filling

1. Wash, destem, and dice the fresh strawberries.

2. Using a mortar and pestle (or a sealed plastic storage bag with a rolling pin), crush the freeze-dried strawberries into a coarse powder.

3. Next, add the crushed strawberries, sugar, lemon zest, and vanilla extract to a small mixing bowl. Gently stir to combine.

To Assemble

1. Line a 9-by-13-inch (22 × 33 cm) baking sheet with parchment paper.

2. Transfer your dough to a large floured cutting board or countertop. Lightly flour a rolling pin and gently roll the dough into a large rectangle about the size of a cookie sheet.

3. Spread 6 tablespoons (85 g) of softened butter evenly over the rolled dough, using a knife or offset spatula.

4. Sprinkle the freeze-dried strawberry/sugar mixture over the dough as evenly as possible, keeping a small border around the edges of the dough (about ½ inch, or 1 cm).

5. Next, sprinkle the fresh strawberries over the sugar mixture.

6. Dollop the strawberry jam around the top of the dough (again, avoiding the edges).

7. Roll up the dough (from the short edge) like a map, as tightly and neatly as you can.

8. Using a sharp knife or my preferred method, a long piece of unflavored dental floss, cut the rolls into 2-inch (5 cm) pieces. (If you're trying the floss method, slip the dental floss under the roll, and every 2 inches draw the floss up, cross over the top, and pull down to the counter. The dental floss will slice through the dough firmly enough for a clean edge, but not hard enough to lose the filling.)

9. Take the cut rolls and nestle them into the prepared baking dish. Repeat the process until you get about 8 rolls. The rolls should be spaced fairly close together.

10. Place a tea towel over the rolls and let them sit somewhere warm for about 60 minutes, for a final rise.

To Bake

1. Preheat the oven to 350°F.

2. After the last rise is complete, place the baking pan on the middle rack and bake for 25 minutes, or until golden brown.

3. Remove from the oven and let cool slightly.

To Make the Elderflower Icing

1. In the bowl of a stand mixer with a whisk attachment, beat the cream cheese and 3 tablespoons (42 g) of butter on medium high for about 5 minutes.

2. Next, add the confectioner's sugar, in two batches, beating between additions.

3. Add the lemon juice, milk, and elderflower liqueur until incorporated. If the icing looks too thick, add another splash of milk.

4. Mix until smooth and lump free (1–2 minutes).

To Finish

Remove the rolls from the baking dish (if desired) and onto a large platter, and drizzle the icing on top.

Serve warm.

MINI CHOCOLATE TRIFLES WITH RASPBERRIES AND CHAMPAGNE WHIPPED CREAM

• Serves 6 •

These preportioned dessert trifles are a breeze to put together. Using homemade or bakery-bought chocolate cake, they are layered with homemade raspberry coulis and champagne-infused whipped cream. Delicate, fruity, and filled with yummy textures, this is a great example of cooking smarter, not harder!

INGREDIENTS

For the Base

2 cups of your favorite chocolate cake
(I like to use my leftover Flourless Chocolate Espresso Cake,
page 48) cubed into roughly 1-inch (3 cm) pieces

For the Raspberry Coulis

12 ounces (340 g) fresh raspberries

½ cup (100 g) sugar

1 tablespoon (15 ml) water

squeeze of fresh lemon juice (about 5 ml)

For the Champagne Whipped Cream

1 cup (240 ml) heavy whipping cream

¼ cup (50 g) sugar

2 tablespoons (10 ml) champagne or sparkling wine (and a
glass for yourself!)

For Garnish

6 ounces (170 g) fresh raspberries

6 ounces (170 g) fresh blackberries

edible flowers such as rose, bachelor's button, borage,
carnation, or dianthus

INSTRUCTIONS

For the Raspberry Coulis

1. Rinse the raspberries and add to a small saucepan with the sugar, water, and a squeeze of fresh lemon juice. Stir to combine.

2. Set the pan on medium-high heat and bring to a boil. Stir occasionally.

3. Let boil for 10 minutes, while stirring with a wooden spoon or spatula to break up the raspberries.

4. Once boiled and slightly thickened, remove from the heat and let cool for 1 minute.

5. Place a fine-mesh sieve over a medium-sized mixing bowl. Pour the raspberry mixture through the sieve and push the cooked fruit through with a rubber spatula.

6. Discard the seeds and the pulp. Transfer the raspberry coulis to a glass jar with a lid. Refrigerate.

For the Champagne Whipped Cream

1. Chill your bowl and whisk attachments for 10 minutes prior to using. In the prechilled mixing bowl, add the heavy whipping cream and beat on medium-high speed until thickened and a little "foamy."

2. Sprinkle in the ¼ cup (50 g) of sugar and beat on high until you see soft peaks (peaks that fall over when you pick up the whisk attachment).

3. Add 2 tablespoons of champagne and beat on high speed until you get medium whipped peaks (peaks that fall over only a little bit when you pick up the whisk!).

To Assemble

1. Using 4 small juice glasses or champagne coupes (4-ounce glass jars work great too!), add 3 cubes of chocolate cake to the bottom of each glass. Press down slightly.

2. Next, drizzle a tablespoon of the chilled raspberry coulis over the cake, followed by a generous spoonful of champagne whipped cream on top.

3. Add a layer of raspberries and blackberries. Press down slightly again.

4. Repeat the layers of chocolate cake and raspberry coulis. Finish with champagne whipped cream on top.

5. Garnish with a few berries and edible flowers

STRAWBERRY SEASON BRUNCH

TABLESCAPE

There's nothing quite like biting into a sun-ripened strawberry! They're red, sweet, and delicious, and I took my inspiration from this classic summer treat. I like to keep my brunches playful and incorporated strawberries across the table. Let's impress your guests with a berry-themed party!

COLOR

A triadic palate of bright reds, clean whites, and touches of yellow and green bring out the lushness of strawberry season!

BLOOMS

Garden roses, white irises, hydrangea, Queen Anne's lace, chamomile flowers, and golden rod create this bountiful floral arrangement. I've added texture with wild rose vines, sprigs of French lavender, and a few wild grape leaves.

THE DETAILS

I really wanted to create a nostalgic scene, so I gathered up a vintage embroidered table runner, and white lace cotton napkins, to set the mood. French, painted, ceramic fruit bowls are filled with fresh ripe strawberries, and the table is sprinkled with antique silver serving pieces from my collection. A green pottery vase holds our bouquet of garden roses. By mixing old with new, we give the table a distinct character for our brunch!

WHAT YOU'LL NEED

*1 large urn-shaped vase with a
    vintage feel*

an array of flowers

*neutral-colored table linens with
    embroidered detailing*

jute twine

*several decorative ceramic bowls to
    hold strawberries*

yellow or amber drinking glasses

blue- or teal-toned dinner plates

ivory salad plates

silver serving pieces

jam jars to hold fresh basil

Set the Table

Location

A shady patio or porch; I've actually used a path alongside my house in this example.

Order of Operations

Spread your white table runner across the length of the table. I have set my larger floral arrangement toward the center of the table, then arranged bowls of strawberries along the table. Each table setting has a dinner plate, a salad plate, and a drinking glass. The cotton napkins are folded into a loose triangle, then, with a length of jute twine, I've tied each napkin with a bow. Place jam jars, full of fresh basil, at intervals near the bowls of fresh strawberries for a pop of color, then add your silver serving pieces.

Small Touches

These garden roses were so gorgeous and plump, I just had to add one rose head to each setting. I snipped the top of each rose, leaving about ½ inch of stem. Then, I tucked each flower into the twine holding the napkins. This small touch was floral, and so chic!

Autumn

I have to be honest: of the four seasons around the table, I think autumn is my favorite! Crisp, cool air, layered with the rich scents of fallen leaves and hickory wood smoke. I love to spend time at the local orchards, picking apples and drinking hot cider with friends. This is the time of year for the warm glow of candlelight on bountiful tables, laughter over cocktails and small bites, and recipes filled with the best of the harvest. Autumn leaves me enchanted with the sleepy, slow honeybees flying back to their hives with the last sips of nectar, and maple trees exploding in a riot of reds, oranges, and golds.

MENUS

FALL HARVEST

APPLE ORANGE BOURBON SOUR
WITH ALLSPICE SIMPLE SYRUP

Unsweetened apple juice meets tart orange and rich bourbon. A homemade allspice simple syrup brings all the fall flavors to this superb riff on a traditional cocktail sour. The allspice simple syrup can be made up to a week in advance.

PEAR AND MANCHEGO CHEESE PUFF PASTRY
TARTS WITH THYME AND HONEY

Savory, sweet, and oh so crispy! A filling made from Spanish Manchego cheese, slices of ripe green pears, thyme, honey, and fresh lavender. This recipe brings the flavors of the orchard right into your kitchen.

HARVEST WALDORF SALAD

A variety of orchard fruits and dried plump dates are mixed with goat cheese and served on a bed of greens. Topped with an aged balsamic vinegar dressing. Sweet, tart, rich, and savory!

SMOKY CHICKEN PAPRIKASH
WITH POTATO MASH

Reproduce the deep flavors of this Hungarian classic comfort meal in an hour! Tender chicken thighs pair gorgeously with a smoky and slightly spicy cream sauce, accompanied by bell peppers, onions, and a hint of garlic. Served over buttery mashed potatoes.

VANILLA CHAI PEAR BUNDT CAKE

A showstopper of a dessert that is ridiculously easy to make. A chai-scented, buttery brown sugar cake, studded with slices of ripe pears and baked until tender. Topped simply with powdered sugar, and you'll have the perfect rustic dessert for your supper party. This cake can be prepared the day before, if desired.

APPLE ORANGE BOURBON SOUR
WITH ALLSPICE SYRUP • Makes one 8-ounce cocktail •

Tangy apple and orange juices create an amazingly refreshing combination that is genuinely among the best bourbon cocktail recipes I've ever made. The key to the deep flavors in this drink is the simple syrup recipe, which uses maple syrup and allspice berries. Sweet, citrusy, and with a hint of spice, this riff off a bourbon sour is a great way to start off your night!

INGREDIENTS

4 ounces (120 ml) filtered unsweetened apple juice

2 ounces (60 ml) bourbon

1 ounce (30 ml) Maple Allspice Simple Syrup (*see right*)

½ ounce (15 ml) freshly squeezed lemon juice

½ ounce (15 ml) freshly squeezed Cara Cara orange juice

2 dashes of Regans' Orange Bitters

ice

for garnish:
citrus wheels, fresh blackberries, or chrysanthemum flowers

INSTRUCTIONS

1. In the cup of a shaker, pour the apple, lemon, and orange juices.

2. Add the bourbon and simple syrup, along with a large handful of ice.

3. Close the shaker and vigorously shake for at least 30 seconds.

4. Take an Old-Fashioned glass or large tumbler and fill halfway with ice.

5. Strain the drink into the glass and add a dash or two of orange bitters.

6. Garnish with a cocktail stick of blackberries, an orange wheel, or chrysanthemum flowers.

Maple Allspice Simple Syrup

A quick cocktail syrup, combining the flavors of real maple syrup, allspice berries, and oranges. Whole allspice berries taste like a combination of all those fall flavors that we love: cinnamon, clove, and nutmeg.

• Makes about 1 cup (240 ml) •

INGREDIENTS

½ cup (120 ml) pure maple syrup

½ cup (100 g) sugar

1 cup (240 ml) water

½ Cara Cara orange sliced
(can also substitute navel oranges)

3 allspice berries

INSTRUCTIONS

1. Place all the ingredients into a small saucepan and set over high heat.

2. Boil for 10 minutes, stirring occasionally.

3. Remove from the heat and strain the simple syrup into a glass jar with fitted top. Discard the solids.

4. Cool before use. The cocktail syrup will last about 2 weeks in the refrigerator.

PEAR AND MANCHEGO CHEESE PUFF PASTRY TARTS
WITH THYME AND HONEY

Quick, easy, and elegant, these individual puff pastry tarts are a great appetizer for any event. Cheese-covered buttery puff pastry rectangles are layered with slices of ripe Bartlett pear, thyme, and coarse sugar. The tart is then baked until golden brown and garnished with honey and fresh lavender blossoms.

INGREDIENTS

1 sheet puff pastry dough

½ cup (90 g) Manchego cheese, shredded

¼ cup (112 g) cream cheese

pinch of kosher salt and ground black pepper

1–2 large (400 g) firm Bartlett pears

1 egg (about 55 g)

1 tablespoon (1.8 g) fresh thyme leaves

1 tablespoon (12 g) raw sugar (optional)

2 tablespoons (42 g) honey for drizzling

2 teaspoons (1.2 g) fresh lavender for garnish

INSTRUCTIONS

1. Preheat the oven to 400°F. Line a large baking sheet with parchment paper.

2. In a small mixing bowl, combine the shredded Manchego cheese, cream cheese, salt, and ground black pepper.

3. Taking the washed pear, cut the flesh away from the core vertically and slice into thin slices, about ⅛ inch (0.25 cm) thick.

4. Spread the puff pastry flat on a large cutting board. With a sharp knife, cut into 6 equal rectangles.

5. Transfer the pastry rectangles to the parchment-covered baking sheet. Using a fork, prick the puff pastry dough several times (this will allow some steam to escape when baking).

6. Next, take about 1 tablespoon of the cheese filling and place in the center of each rectangle. Using a knife (or your fingers), spread the cheese slightly, leaving about a ¾-inch (20 mm) border of dough around the edges.

7. Fan out 3 thin slices of pear on each pastry.

8. Take a small bowl and whisk the egg. Using a pastry brush, spread the whisked egg along the border of each pastry (avoiding the pear and cheese). This will give the pastry edges a golden and shiny finish after baking.

9. Sprinkle fresh thyme leaves (and optionally, raw sugar as well) over each puff pastry rectangle.

10. Before baking, place the pan directly into the refrigerator to chill slightly (about 10 minutes). The pastry will "puff" much more evenly if it's cold throughout.

11. After chilling, place the pan directly into the hot oven for 25 minutes or until golden.

12. Remove and cool lightly on wire rack.

13. Transfer to a platter (the pastry can be cut into triangles if smaller portions are desired.)

14. Drizzle with honey and fresh lavender before serving.

HARVEST WALDORF SALAD

• Serves 6 •

This salad recipe is an autumn play on a classic Waldorf salad. It contains a delicious mix of crunchy pecans, crisp apples, sweet dates, and juicy grapes, tossed with goat milk chèvre over wild greens and a balsamic dressing.

INGREDIENTS

For the Salad

1 large (200 g) Granny Smith apple
(this adds tartness and texture)

1 large (200 g) gala or honeycrisp apple
(this adds sweetness and texture)

1 cup (150 g) red grapes

1 cup (160 g) pitted dried dates

¾ cup (85 g) pecan halves

4 ounces (112 g) chèvre (soft goat cheese)

3 cups (90 g) mixed baby greens

wedge of lemon

For the Balsamic Dressing

¼ cup (60 ml) aged balsamic vinegar

2 tablespoons (30 ml) extra-virgin olive oil

2 teaspoons (10 g) Dijon mustard

2 teaspoons (14 g) honey

kosher salt and ground black pepper

INSTRUCTIONS

For the Salad Base

1. Rinse and dry the apples, grapes, and greens. Take each apple and cut into ½-inch (1 cm) cubes (discarding the core), placing cubes into a large mixing bowl. Give the apples a small squirt of lemon juice and toss (this is to prevent browning).

2. Halve the grapes and slice the dates into thirds (the pieces should be roughly the same size as the pieces of apple). Add to the bowl.

3. Roughly chop the pecans into thirds and combine with the fruit.

4. Take the chèvre and break into several chunks. Add to the bowl and mix well to combine. This should coat all the ingredients.

For the Dressing

1. Whisk all the ingredients in a small bowl and add salt and pepper to taste.

2. Using individual salad plates, take about a ½ cup (15 g) of washed salad greens and slightly mound. Gently spoon the preferred amount of balsamic dressing on the greens. Place a generous helping of the fruit/nut mixture over the top.

SMOKY CHICKEN PAPRIKASH
WITH POTATO MASH · Serves 6 ·

This Hungarian-inspired chicken paprikash (paprika chicken) shows off the full-bodied flavors of smoked paprika and garlic, combined with bell peppers, shallots, sour cream, and savory chicken thighs. This variation is easy enough to make for a weeknight dinner without losing the deep flavors you would expect of a dish simmered for hours. The key to this dish? Using smoked paprika instead of the traditional sweet or hot paprika; it adds an umami note, and lots of depth to this savory one-pan chicken recipe!

INGREDIENTS

3 + 3 tablespoons (24 g + 24 g) all-purpose flour, divided

1½ tablespoons (15 g) + ½ teaspoon (1.6 g) smoked paprika, divided

6 boneless, skinless chicken thighs (about 500 g)

kosher salt

ground black pepper

2 tablespoons (30 ml) extra-virgin olive oil

4 cloves (20 g) fresh garlic, minced

3 large (120 g) shallots, minced

1 red bell pepper (150 g), chopped

1 yellow bell pepper (150 g), chopped

3 tablespoons (42 g) butter

½ teaspoon (1.6 g) ground cumin

1½ cups (355 ml) chicken stock

½ cup (120 g) sour cream

freshly chopped Italian parsley for garnish

Creamy Mashed Potatoes for serving (*see page 142*)

INSTRUCTIONS

For the Chicken

1. Add 3 tablespoons (24 g) flour and ½ teaspoon (1.6 g) smoked paprika to a plate. Mix with a fork to distribute evenly.

2. Gently pat dry the chicken thighs. Season both sides of the chicken with salt and black pepper, then dredge the chicken in the seasoned flour.

3. Preheat a large Dutch oven, or cast-iron skillet, over medium heat. Add 2 tablespoons (30 ml) olive oil to the pot.

4. Once heated and slightly foamy, start to sear your chicken in batches. We want to brown and *partly* cook the chicken, for about 4 minutes on each side (This is less than fully cooked. The chicken will finish cooking when added to the sauce).

5. After this is cooked, place the chicken on a plate and reserve. Keep the oil in the pan for the next stage.

For the Sauce

1. Using the same Dutch oven or skillet that you used to cook the chicken, add your minced garlic. Let cook while stirring until fragrant.

2. Next, add in the diced peppers and shallots, with a hefty pinch of kosher salt. Stir and cook until slightly softened (about 5 minutes.)

3. Now, to make the roux: push the cooked vegetables to one side of the pot and add 3 tablespoons (42 g) of butter. Heat until foamy.

4. Add the 3 tablespoons (24 g) of flour over the liquid butter and stir the flour/butter continuously. (Try to keep the veggies to one side of the pot, but don't panic if a few escape!)

5. Cook the roux until it becomes a nutty brown (about 3 minutes).

6. Once it's light brown in color, mix the cooked veggies into the roux and add the remainder of the smoked paprika, along with ½ teaspoon of cumin. Mix.

7. Pour the chicken stock into this mix. Stir while heating, until thickened (about 4 minutes).

8. Add the chicken back into the sauce, along with ½ cup (120 g) of sour cream. Mix gently. Adjust the salt and pepper to taste.

9. Let simmer on low for 5 minutes to finish the chicken and meld the flavors.

10. Serve over mashed potatoes (though it also pairs well with noodles or rice).

11. Garnish with fresh flat parsley.

CREAMY MASHED POTATOES · Serves 6–8 ·

My favorite starchy side dish, these mashed potatoes are super-creamy and buttery. I prefer to use Yukon Gold potatoes, since they cook quickly and have the most amazing texture, but you can use any potato variety you like. My trick for making super-smooth mashed potatoes? A potato ricer. This handy tool transforms boiled potatoes by pressing them through a filter with many small holes. The result is a potato so fine that it melts into the butter and cream. Although every mashed-potato recipe calls for a different amount of cream and butter, this is the ratio I prefer to use.

INGREDIENTS

6 large (1,000 g) Yukon Gold potatoes, peeled and cut into eighths

water

salt

⅓ cup (80 ml) half-and-half or light cream

4 tablespoons (56 g) butter (room temperature)

ground black pepper

special equipment:
a potato ricer

INSTRUCTIONS

1. Add the peeled and cut potatoes to a large pot and fill with enough cold water to just cover the potatoes. Add a generous pinch of salt and set on high heat.

2. Bring to a boil and cook until the potatoes are tender (about 15 minutes).

3. Drain the cooked potatoes and push them through your potato ricer and back into the large pot.

4. In a separate pot on the stove over medium heat (or in a nonmetallic bowl in the microwave), gently heat the dairy products until the butter is melted.

5. Add the melted butter / half-and-half to the "riced" potatoes. Stir with a large wooden spoon until incorporated. If the potatoes seem a little dry, you can add another tablespoon of melted butter.

6. Salt and pepper to taste.

VANILLA CHAI PEAR BUNDT CAKE

• Serves 10 •

This autumn pear dessert is so delicious, and approachable for even a novice baker. Real ground chai lends this dessert the incredible fragrances of cardamon, nutmeg, ginger, and clove. To heighten the sweetness of the juicy pears and the dramatic appearance, we'll top this cake with a quick dusting of powdered sugar.

INGREDIENTS

1 tablespoon (4.5 g) fine chai

2 sticks (225 g) butter, room temperature

1 cup (200 g) sugar

¼ cup (30 g) brown sugar

4 eggs (about 220 g), room temperature

2 teaspoons (9.6 g) fine vanilla extract

3 cups (385 g) all-purpose flour

1 teaspoon (4.5 g) baking powder

½ teaspoon (2.2 g) baking soda

½ teaspoon (1.5 g) salt

1 teaspoon (2.5 g) ground cinnamon

1 cup (237 ml) whole milk

2 Bartlett pears (about 500 g)

2 tablespoons (16 g) powdered sugar for garnish

INSTRUCTIONS

1. Preheat the oven to 350°F and place a rack in the middle.

2. Take the chai tea and grind in a spice grinder or with a mortar and pestle.

3. In the bowl of a stand mixer with the paddle attachment, cream together the butter, sugar, brown sugar, and ground chai on medium-high speed for about 5 minutes.

4. After beating the butter and sugar, add the eggs one at a time, making sure to beat in completely before adding the next. Scrape down the sides with a spatula as needed.

5. Add the vanilla extract and beat to mix.

6. In a separate large bowl, fork-mix the flour, baking powder, baking soda, salt, and cinnamon.

7. Lowering the speed, begin to alternate adding a quarter of the dry ingredients from the bowl with about a quarter of the milk. Repeat this until out of milk and dry ingredients (I start and end with the flour mixture). Beat until well mixed.

8. Using the wax wrappers of the butter sticks, lightly grease the entire inside of the Bundt pan. Make sure to get into every nook and cranny. (Alternatively, you can use a baking spray.)

9. Add 1–2 teaspoons of flour to the Bundt pan, then gently tap to spread the flour throughout. Invert the pan and tap any excess flour out. This extra layer should help the cake come out of the pan smoothly.

10. Wash and dry the pears. Cut into ⅛-inch-thick (0.25 cm) vertical slices, cutting as close to the core as possible—the slices should resemble cross sections of the pear itself.

11. Taking the Bundt pan, spoon a layer of batter (about 1 inch, or 2.5 cm) evenly around the bottom, smoothing it lightly with a spoon or rubber spatula.

12. Take the pear slices, with the narrow end pointing down, and sink them into the batter. (I like to fit each slice into a groove of the Bundt mold. The goal here is to have a slice of pear with every slice of cake!)

13. Once the pear slices have been arranged, begin to evenly spoon the rest of the batter into the pan. Gently place the batter between the pear slices with a spoon, then place batter over the top with an offset spatula or large spoon.

14. On a cutting board, firmly tap (bang!) the pan down a few times to help get rid of any air bubbles that may be trapped.

15. Place the Bundt cake into the preheated oven and cook for 50–60 minutes, or until a skewer comes out clean from the cake.

16. Let cool on a wire rack for 10–15 minutes and then invert to remove from the cake mold.

17. Cool completely before topping with powdered sugar.

 GF Replace the all-purpose flour with *Bob's Red Mill Gluten Free 1-to-1 Baking Flour.*

FALL HARVEST

TABLESCAPE

It's autumn, and the trees are going to sleep, ending the growing season in a conflagration of red, orange, and gold. It's time for trips to the apple orchard, and cool nights in front of a fire pit. We'll soak in all the vibrant fall colors and set the table for a beautiful harvest feast!

COLOR

We're using an analogous color scheme for our harvest table flowers. Bright purple, orange, and reds will be the primary focus, with touches of green, yellow, and blue from our table decor.

BLOOMS

Bright-purple lisianthus, orange garden roses, and red roses are accented with lacy Queen Anne's lace and stalks of millet. Bunches of wild grapes and leaves bring a foraged, seasonal element.

WHAT YOU'LL NEED

1 silvered glass compote vase

4 small jam jars

assorted and grasses

a neutral-colored table runner with embroidered details

burnt-orange and sage-green linen napkins

gold-toned napkin rings

3-tier cupcake stand

basket-weave place mats

several vintage mismatched sets of dinner and salad plates

amber- or yellow-colored goblets

2 taller candlesticks with tapers

4 smaller glass votives and votive candles

gold- or brass-toned objects d'art, or small decor pieces such as stars, orbs, or organic shapes.

assorted fall fruits such as apples, pomegranates, pears, grapes, and black plums

THE DETAILS

Antique French cast-iron candlesticks are outfitted with artisan tapers in sage green and dusty blue. Our floral centerpiece design is wild and free, reflecting the feeling of the natural backdrop. We'll use muted-green and burnt-orange napkins, and a neutral-colored table runner with embroidered details. Mismatched antique place settings give a touch of whimsy, while maintaining elegance at our harvest table. We will brighten the scene with amber-colored glass votives and goblets.

Set the Table

Location

A large dining room, patio, or shady lawn (weather permitting!).

Order of Operations

Lay a neutral-colored table runner across the length of the surface and set the large harvest floral centerpiece in the center. I have used tall candlesticks with tapers on either side of the floral centerpiece, then added small votive candles and jars of flowers across the table, focusing on filling in any blank spaces. Decorative objects can be clustered around the votives or floral jam jars. Here, I have placed a cupcake stand filled with fall fruits and flowers on one end of the table. Each table setting consists of silverware, accompanied by a charger, dinner plate, salad plate, napkin, and goblet.

Small Touches

I've incorporated several small touches, foraged from my yard, into this table. Red crabapples are clustered around the cake and smaller floral arrangements. I've also inserted a stalk of dried wheat into each napkin, for a textural touch. To amp up the fall mood, I've also filled a three-tier cupcake stand with assorted fruits, and flowers of the season.

ENCHANTED COCKTAIL PARTY

BUTTERFLY PEA BLOSSOM CRANBERRY
GIN SOUR

Sweet and tart, this color-changing cocktail has a secret "magical" ingredient: homemade butterfly pea blossom simple syrup! Complemented with floral gin and white cranberry juice. The simple syrup can be made up to a week in advance.

TEMPTING FALL CHARCUTERIE BOARD

The easiest way to serve appetizers to a hungry crowd, this charcuterie board stuns with savory cured Italian meats and sausages, hard cheeses, dried fruits, and a cranberry relish.

POACHED WHITE FISH WITH SWISS CHARD
IN SPICY MUSHROOM BROTH

Upscale doesn't have to mean fussy! All the deep, earthy flavors of late autumn combine in this dish, and we'll use some time-saving cooking techniques to "set it and forget it." The mushroom broth can be made the day before, if desired.

IRISH APPLE CAKE WITH
VANILLA-DARJEELING CUSTARD SAUCE

An elevated classic: layers of juicy apples sit on top of a tender butter cake. Baked until golden and served with a vanilla-and-tea-infused custard sauce. This cake can be made the day before, but the custard is best made the day of your event.

BUTTERFLY PEA BLOSSOM CRANBERRY GIN SOUR

Dried butterfly pea blossoms are a truly interesting way to make any cocktail special. They can be used as a garnish or, even better, to create a unique cocktail syrup. The extract from this flower colors the simple syrup a bright blue but changes to a lovely soft pink when you add acid!

Note: We'll be using this syrup in a classic egg-white-foam gin sour. I know what you're thinking: Raw plus egg? Yes! Make sure you use a fresh egg white, and you're safe to go. After shaking, the egg white turns into a delightful velvety foam that complements the tart white cranberry juice. Believe me, this is a truly enchanted cocktail!

INGREDIENTS

2 ounces (60 ml) gin with floral notes (such as Hendrick's)

1 ounce (30 ml) fresh lemon juice

1 ounce (30 ml) white cranberry juice

¾ ounce (22 ml) Butterfly Pea Blossom Simple Syrup
(*see page 150*)

½ ounce (15 ml) elderflower liqueur

1 egg white
(30 ml aquafaba can be substituted if an egg is not desired)

pinch of salt

ice

for garnish: food-safe dried rosebuds

149

INSTRUCTIONS

1. Pour the gin, white cranberry juice, lemon juice, elderflower liqueur, and butterfly pea blossom simple syrup into ½ of a shaker.

2. Crack a fresh egg and separate out the white (you will not need the yolk for this recipe; use it to make a sabayon, like the one on page 216!); add the egg white to the shaker. Substitute with the aquafaba if not using egg.

3. Add a few grains of kosher salt to the cup (this heightens the flavors!).

4. Add a generous handful of ice and close the top of the shaker.

5. Shake vigorously for 45 seconds, or until frothy.

6. Using a cocktail strainer, strain the drink into a chilled coupe glass.

7. Garnish with edible dried rosebuds and enjoy!

Note on aquafaba: This is the liquid found in a can of chickpeas, but it can also be purchased separately. This vegan alternative has several proteins that mimic the frothing qualities of an egg white.

Butterfly Pea Blossom Simple Syrup

• Makes 1 cup •

INGREDIENTS

1 cup (237 ml) water

1 cup (200 g) sugar

1 tablespoon (3 g) food-grade dried butterfly pea blossom flowers

INSTRUCTIONS

1. In a small pot, combine all the ingredients and give a quick stir.

2. Set over high heat and let to come to a boil.

3. Let boil for 5 minutes and then remove from the heat.

4. Strain the syrup into a clean, sealable jar, using a sieve. Discard the solids.

5. Store covered in the refrigerator for up to two weeks.

TEMPTING FALL
CHARCUTERIE BOARD

• Serves 12 •

A charcuterie board is simply a collection of smoked or cured meats, fish, or even patés. I also like to add an array of cheeses, fruits, pickled vegetables, and mustards. Small sweets, nuts, and jams are also wonderful for making a mix-and-match taste adventure. Serve with crusty bread or crackers on the side, for the perfect grazing plate.

INGREDIENTS

2–3 cured meats (50–100 g of each),
such as thick-cut (cooked) bacon, salumi, prosciutto, or
smoked beef sausage

2–3 aged cheeses (100 g each),
from different regions, such as Spanish Manchego
and Italian Artigiano
(you are going for contrasts, but also consider ease of
consumption, so firm cheeses are a help!)

3 tablespoons (45 g) Dijon mustard

⅓ cup (100 g) fruit jam or relish, such as c
ranberry sauce or fig jam

¼ cup (50 g) pepperoncini peppers

½ cup (80 g) fresh blackberries

¼ cup (40 g) dried cherries

⅓ cup (50 g) dried figs

⅓ cup (50 g) dried medjool dates

½ cup (60 g) dried apricots

½ cup (60 g) raw pecan halves

4–6 (50 g) dark chocolate squares

1–2 (120 g) clementines

fresh herbs, such as basil leaves and
sprigs of rosemary

edible flowers such as cosmos, dahlia, or fennel flower

crusty bread and crackers

INSTRUCTIONS

1. Wash and dry all the fresh fruits and herbs.

2. Using a large platter, first arrange your small finger bowls of condiments, pickled peppers, and blocks of cheese at intervals.

3. Fold or roll your meats and add to the plate. Fill in the gaps with a mix of dried fruits, fresh berries, nuts, clementines, and chocolate. Think big and bountiful!

4. Garnish with fresh herbs.

POACHED WHITE FISH
WITH SWISS CHARD IN SPICY MUSHROOM BROTH

• Serves 4 •

Earthy, spicy, and mildly sweet, this dried shiitake mushroom broth elevates the flavors of the fish, while crispy shallots provide a touch of crunch. Sauteed greens counterpoint the delicate flavors.

INGREDIENTS

For the Fish

16 ounces (450 g) white fish, such as Atlantic cod or sea bass

3 tablespoons (45 g) butter

Pinch (about 1.2 g) kosher salt

special equipment:
sous vide immersion cooker

For the Shiitake Mushroom Broth

3 cups (720 ml) high-quality vegetable broth

½ ounce (14 g) dried shiitake mushrooms

half (10 g) a red Fresno or jalapeño pepper

2 green scallions (40 g) + more for garnish

pinch of kosher salt

freshly ground black pepper

For the Sauteed Bitter Greens

5 ounces (140 g) fresh baby spinach or chard
(Swiss chard is more assertively bitter than spinach)

1 tablespoon (15 ml) extra-virgin olive oil

½ teaspoon (2 g) garlic powder

pinch (about 1.2 g) kosher salt

freshly ground black pepper

½ teaspoon (2.5 ml) fresh lemon juice

For the Crisped Shallots

1 large (80 g) shallot, peeled and cut into thin rings

3 tablespoons (45 ml) extra-virgin olive oil

INSTRUCTIONS

For the Fish

There are many ways to prepare fish, but for this dish I prefer this butter-poaching method, which uses a sous vide:

1. Trim your fish into 4-ounce (115 g) portions, season with salt, and place into a heat-safe sous vide bag, along with the butter.

2. Seal the bag and place in a sous vide bath set to 130°F (54°C) for 30–45 minutes. Remove fish when ready.

Note: If you prefer a traditional butter poach on a stovetop, clarify enough butter to cover the fish, then simmer in butter for about 10 minutes.

For the Shiitake Mushroom Broth

1. In a medium-sized pot, combine the vegetable broth and dried shiitake mushrooms. Place over high heat and bring to a boil. Once at a boil, lower the temperature to a simmer and cover with a lid. Let cook for 30 minutes.

2. Slice the pepper (remove the seeds if you prefer a less spicy broth). Trim two green scallions and cut in thirds.

3. Uncover the mushroom broth and add the scallions and chili, allowing to simmer for 5 minutes.

4. Remove from the heat and strain the scallions, chili, and mushrooms from the broth. Add the strained broth back to the pot to keep warm.

For the Sauteed Bitter Greens

1. Wash and dry your greens. Place a large skillet over medium heat, add the olive oil, and let heat until shimmery.

2. Add the greens to the skillet with the salt, pepper, and garlic powder. Let cook for 3–5 minutes, while stirring. Watch that you don't brown the greens; we are looking for wilting rather than searing.

3. After wilting, add the lemon juice and stir. Cook 30 seconds. Remove from the heat and reserve.

For the Crisped Shallots

1. Peel and slice the shallot into thin rings. Heat 3 tablespoons of extra-virgin olive oil in a skillet and place over medium-high heat. Prepare a plate with several sheets of paper towels to drain the shallots.

2. Once the oil is hot, you will shallow-fry the shallots. Add the shallots to the pan and stir gently, allowing them to fry until crispy and brown. About 5 minutes.

3. Once they're fried, transfer the shallots to the plate with the paper towels to drain.

To Assemble

1. Reserve four shallow bowls or small pasta bowls.

2. Add a portion of white fish to the center of the bowl, Pour ¼ cup (80 ml) of the mushroom broth along the side of each bowl, being careful not to splash the top of the fish. Top the poached white fish with the crispy shallots and a scattering of sliced scallion rings.

3. Add a spoonful of wilted greens next to the fish. (Leaving the greens in contact with the broth will eventually cause the broth to absorb some of the bitterness of the greens. This can be prevented by either adding the greens immediately before serving, or plating the dish without broth, then adding it to the dish once at the table.)

4. Serve immediately.

IRISH APPLE CAKE
WITH VANILLA-DARJEELING CUSTARD SAUCE

• Serves 10 •

A beautifully simple fall dessert that packs a big apple-flavored punch! Buttery cake is layered with juicy honeycrisp apples and covered with an oatmeal crumble. Topped with a classic Darjeeling tea-infused custard, this is a sweet treat to end any meal.

INGREDIENTS

For the Custard

1½ cups (355 ml) whole milk

1 teabag (3 g) fine Darjeeling tea (to be brewed)

¼ cup (50 g) granulated sugar

6 egg yolks

1 teaspoon (4.8 g) vanilla extract

For the Crumble Topping

¾ cup (100 g) all-purpose flour

⅓ cup (27 g) old-fashioned rolled oats

½ cup (100 g) granulated sugar

6 tablespoons (85 g) cold unsalted butter, cut into cubes

pinch of kosher salt

For the Cake Batter

½ cup (115 g) unsalted butter, at room temperature

½ cup (100 g) granulated sugar

2 large eggs (about 110g), at room temperature

3 tablespoons (45 ml) heavy cream

1¼ cups (160 g) all-purpose flour

1 teaspoon (2.5 g) ground cinnamon

1 teaspoon (4.5 g) baking soda

1 pinch (1.2 g) kosher salt

4 honeycrisp apples (about 800 g), peeled

1 tablespoon (14 g) butter, for greasing the pan

3 tablespoons (24 g) powdered sugar, to top

special equipment:
1 9-inch (23 cm) round springform pan

INSTRUCTIONS

For the Custard

1. Add the milk to a medium-sized pot and submerge the bag of tea into it. Heat the milk on medium heat, until steaming, but be careful not to scald. Stir occasionally.

2. Once the milk has reached temperature, remove from the heat and discard the teabag.

3. In a large bowl, whisk the sugar and egg yolks together until blended.

4. To temper the eggs, slowly ladle the tea / hot milk mixture into the eggs, in a thin stream, while whisking vigorously. The slow addition of hot milk will gently bring the eggs up to temperature without scrambling them. Continue to slowly ladle until about half of the milk is incorporated. Keep whisking!

5. Once half of the milk is incorporated, pour the liquid in the bowl into the milk on the stove and continue to whisk. Cook on medium heat and change to stirring with a rubber spatula. The goal is constant heat, not "quick and hot," while making this custard.

6. Continue stirring until the liquid thickens enough to coat the back of the spatula. Remove from the heat and stir in the vanilla extract.

7. Using a fine-mesh sieve placed over a small mixing bowl, strain the custard of any leftover egg curd.

8. Cover the custard (if using plastic wrap, place the sheet right onto the surface of the strained custard, to prevent a "skin" from forming while cooling.) Refrigerate until use.

For the Crumble

1. In a medium-sized mixing bowl, add the flour, oats, sugar, salt, and butter cubes.

2. Work the butter into the dry mixture with your fingers (the heat of your hands will help incorporate the butter and dry ingredients together).

3. Mix and "squish" the butter, until a rough, sandy texture is reached. Place the crumble in the refrigerator to chill until the cake batter is ready.

For the Cake

1. Preheat the oven to 350°F.

2. Line the springform pan with a circle of parchment paper at the bottom, and butter the sides. Reserve.

3. Peel and core the apples. Slice into thin pieces (about ⅛ inch, or 0.25 cm) and place into a large mixing bowl.

4. In the bowl of a stand beater, cream the butter and sugar until light and fluffy (about 4 minutes). Scrape down the bowl periodically.

5. Add the eggs one at a time, while mixing on medium speed.

6. In a large bowl, add all the dry ingredients and fork-stir.

7. Alternate adding the dry mix and the 3 tablespoons (45 ml) of heavy cream into the butter/eggs/sugar mixture on medium speed, until you get a thick batter. Scrape the sides of the bowl as needed.

8. Spoon the batter into the prepared springform pan and smooth into an even layer with an offset spatula or spoon.

9. Add all the apple slices in an even layer over the batter. (This will look like a lot of fruit, but don't worry; it will cook properly and be delicious!)

10. Sprinkle the crumble topping evenly on top of the apple layer, then place the cake into the oven.

11. Bake for 50 minutes, or until a toothpick comes out cleanly from the center of the cake. The topping should be slightly browned and golden.

12. Let cool on a baking rack for 10–15 minutes before serving.

13. Pop from the springform pan and dust with powdered sugar.

14. Slice into portions and drizzle the custard overtop as desired.

GROWN-UP TRICK-OR-TREAT

TABLESCAPE

There's a certain magic in the air! The weather may be crisp, and the days short, but the local harvest fruits are juicy and ripe. It's time to throw an enchanted fall cocktail party to celebrate the season. Create a magical, mysterious mood, with bright florals, luscious bites, golden candlelight, and lots of small touches that provide big impact! Who wouldn't want to sip on an enchanted brew at this table?

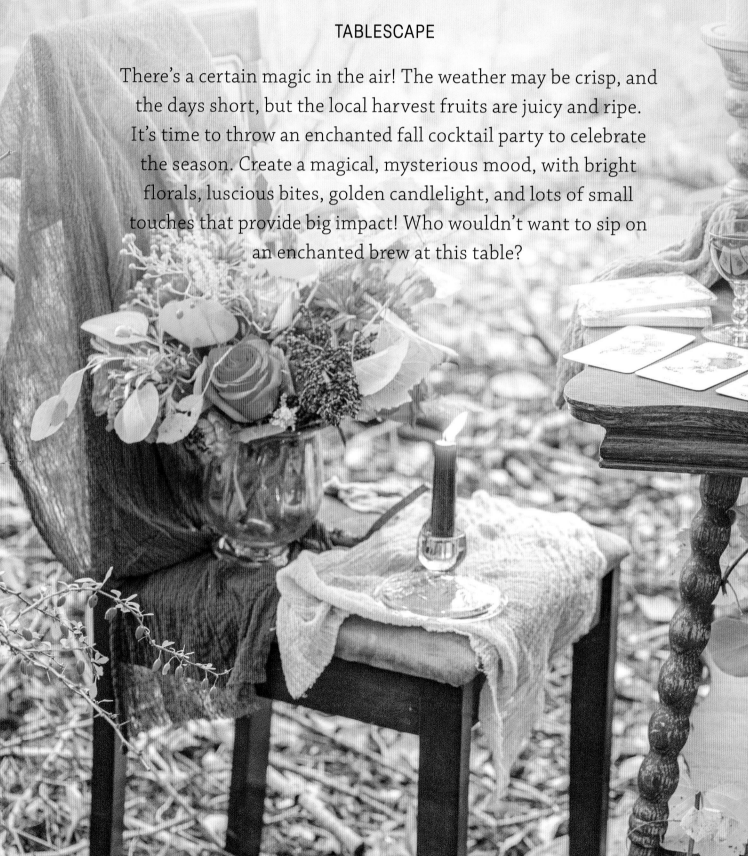

COLOR

I chose to use an analogous color palette to reflect the majesty of the season: deep reds, magenta, purples, and pinks, accented with orange, yellow, and green.

BLOOMS

Chrysanthemums, roses, lilies, carnation, eryngium, and allium make up the bulk of this arrangement. I've added autumn wildflowers, such as goldenrod and witches' broom, to bring out some texture, as well as silver dollar eucalyptus.

THE DETAILS

Glass and wooden candlesticks hold textured beeswax candles. Baskets and bowls filled with pears, plums, and apples dot the table. Flashes of white marble contrast with the deep red of pomegranates. Rosemary bundles and a blue linen runner anchor the scene.peonies and delicate irises.

WHAT YOU'LL NEED

1 large, short cylinder vase + 1 medium urn-shaped vase

assorted flowers and grasses

2 yards of colorful cheesecloth or linen; I used a dusty-blue tone

a variety of small pedestals and cake stands

small stemmed cocktail glasses

woven baskets to hold fruit

candlesticks of various heights and materials

beeswax pillars and colored tapered candles

pumpkins, decorative gourds, and vines

fresh sprigs of woody herbs like rosemary and sage

satin or velvet ribbon

a tarot deck if you're feeling it!

Set the Table

Location

A forest, garden, or backyard.

Order of Operations

Drape your linen runner or cheese cloth across the length of the table. Gently bunch several sections up to create a water-like effect. Place the largest items in sets of three. These include the candlesticks, flower arrangements, and fruit baskets, as well as loose fruits. Place your cake stands in open spots and top them with fruits, gourds, and flowers.

Small Touches

Wrap herb bundles with ribbon, tuck the edges underneath, and lay them on the table as decorative elements. Set out plenty of little plates with fruits, cheese, and sweets. Have your cocktails at the ready, and light your candles.

GROWN-UP TRICK-OR-TREAT SUPPER

CIDER AND WHISKEY BOULEVARDIER

A "no shake" spiced whiskey cocktail with hints of orange, apple cider, and cinnamon. My favorite drink to serve around a bonfire. The cinnamon syrup can be made up to a week in advance.

BLACK LENTIL SALAD WITH TOMATOES, CUCUMBERS, AND MINT

Toothsome black lentils are given some Mediterranean flair, with bright mint, tomatoes, cucumbers, dill, and olive oil. The lentils can be made the day before.

ROASTED HEAD OF CAULIFLOWER WITH ZA'ATAR, HONEYED CHERRIES, AND TAHINI

Tender whole-roasted cauliflower is seasoned with this Middle Eastern spice blend and complemented with marinated sweet cherries and a tangy sesame sauce. The marinated cherries can be made up to a week in advance, and the tahini sauce can be made the day before your event.

CRISPY SMASHED BABY POTATOES WITH GARLIC, HERBS, AND FETA CHEESE

The best crispy potato you've ever eaten! Boiled, pressed, and then coated with a generous portion of olive oil. Baked until super crispy and then with fresh herbs, garlic, and tangy feta cheese.

PUMPKIN PRETZEL BLONDIES WITH CHOCOLATE CANDIES

We can't let the kids have all the fun! A pumpkin-filled dessert bar, studded with candy-coated chocolates and crunchy pretzel pieces. A nostalgic blondie recipe both for kids and the kid at heart. The blondies can be made the day before your event.

CIDER AND WHISKEY BOULEVARDIER

• Makes one 6-ounce cocktail •

Although it sounds complicated, a boulevardier is pretty much a Negroni, but with whiskey replacing the gin. It's a classic stirred cocktail in the same family as an Old-Fashioned. This drink combines the charm of apple cider with a homemade cinnamon simple syrup, tart Campari, sweet vermouth, and smoky whiskey. Simply combine all the ingredients into the cup of a cocktail shaker, add a bit of ice, and stir for the perfect fireside sipper.

INGREDIENTS

1½ ounces (45 ml) rye whiskey

½ ounce (15 ml) Campari

½ ounce (15 ml) sweet vermouth

1 ounce (30 ml) apple cider

½ ounce (15 ml) Cinnamon Simple Syrup
(*see right*)

squeeze of fresh orange

twist of orange

ice

for garnish (optional): orange wheels, orange twists,
or food-grade fresh marigolds

INSTRUCTIONS

1. Pour all the liquids + squeeze of orange into a cocktail shaker or mixing glass.

2. Add a handful of ice. Stir gently with a cocktail spoon.

3. Strain over ice into your favorite Old-Fashioned or rocks glass.

4. Expel some orange zest over the glass to release the oils.

5. Garnish as desired with orange wheels or twists, and fresh marigolds.

Cinnamon Simple Syrup

A delicious sugar syrup that's as tasty in your morning coffee as it is in your evening cocktails!

• Makes about ½ cup (125 ml) •

INGREDIENTS

½ cup (118 ml) water

½ cup (60 g) brown sugar

⅛ teaspoon (0.3 g) ground cinnamon

INSTRUCTIONS

1. Combine the ½ cup of water, ½ cup brown sugar, and ⅛ teaspoon of ground cinnamon in a small pot and set over high heat to a boil.

2. Let boil 5 minutes.

3. Remove from the heat.

4. Let cool to room temperature and store in a sealed jar in the refrigerator.

5. The syrup will be good for up to 2 weeks.

BLACK LENTIL SALAD WITH TOMATOES, CUCUMBERS, AND MINT

Inspired by the flavors of the Middle East and Mediterranean, this side salad features global flavors to excite your guests! Toothsome black beluga lentils are boiled with bay leaf and garlic, for an earthy base. Acidic tomatoes, cool cucumbers, bright fresh herbs, and a bit of red onion round out the flavor. Tossed with a bit of red wine vinegar and olive oil, this is a salad recipe that fills you up like a main dish.

INGREDIENTS

1 cup (200 g) beluga black lentils

2½ cups (about 600 ml) water

1 clove (5 g) garlic, peeled

1 dried bay leaf

1 cup (150 g) grape tomatoes

½ red (75 g) bell pepper

1 small cucumber (about 150 g)

¼ (50 g) red onion

½ cup (5 g) fresh mint, packed

¼ cup (2.5 g) fresh dill, packed

¼ cup (2.5 g) fresh Italian parsley leaves, packed

½ lemon, juiced (15 ml juice)

1 tablespoon (15 ml) extra-virgin olive oil

1 tablespoon (15 ml) red wine vinegar

½ teaspoon (1.2 g) Za'atar

kosher salt

freshly ground black pepper

INSTRUCTIONS

1. Rinse the lentils under cold water in a sieve and carefully pick through for any small stones.

2. In a small pot, add the lentils to the cold water, along with the garlic clove, a heavy pinch of salt, and a bay leaf. Place on medium-high heat and bring to a boil.

3. Once boiling, turn the temperature down to a simmer. Let cook, uncovered, for about 20 minutes, or until the lentils are tender and the cooking liquid has evaporated. If the water boils down before the lentils are ready, add a small splash more to the pot.

4. After cooking, remove from the heat, discarding the bay leaf and garlic, and allow the lentils to cool.

5. Slice the grape tomatoes in half and then dice the red onion, bell pepper, and cucumbers. The goal is to have all the vegetables roughly the same size. Wash and dry the fresh herbs and either hand-tear them or roughly chop with a knife.

6. Taking a large bowl, add all the vegetables and herbs, along with the cooked lentils.

7. Drizzle in the lemon juice, red wine vinegar, olive oil, and Za'atar.

8. Stir well to combine, then add salt and pepper to taste.

9. Cover the bowl and let sit in the refrigerator for at least 15 minutes before serving, for the flavors to meld.

ROASTED HEAD OF CAULIFLOWER
WITH ZA'ATAR, HONEYED CHERRIES, AND TAHINI

• Serves 8–10 •

This highly seasoned whole head of cauliflower is absolutely packed full of flavor! Cooked at a high heat, the cauliflower comes out steaming and tender. The bold spices of the Za'atar (a traditional Middle Eastern spice mixture that includes thyme, sumac, oregano, salt, and sesame seeds) pair with the soft, almost creamy, cauliflower and, when combined with sweet marinated red cherries and tahini sauce, makes for one stunning entrée.

INGREDIENTS

For the Cauliflower

1 medium to large head of cauliflower (about 1,000 g)

1 cup (240 ml) water

1 teaspoon (3 g) kosher salt

1 tablespoon (7 g) Za'atar

¼ teaspoon (0.8 g) spoked paprika

freshly ground black pepper

2 teaspoons (30 ml) fresh lemon juice

2 tablespoons (30 ml) + 2 tablespoons (30 ml) extra-virgin olive oil, divided

special equipment:

large baking tray or cast-iron skillet

aluminum foil

For the Honeyed Cherries

½ cup (100 g) fresh red cherries

1 tablespoon (15 ml) extra-virgin olive oil

1 tablespoon (15 ml) red wine vinegar

1 tablespoon (21 g) honey

pinch (0.4 g) ground cinnamon

pinch (1.2 g) kosher salt

For the Tahini Sauce

¼ cup (60 g) tahini

½ lemon, juiced (15 ml juice)

1 tablespoon (15 ml) extra-virgin olive oil

2 tablespoons (10 g) chopped Italian parsley +
more for garnish

pinch (1.2 g) kosher salt

freshly ground black pepper

INSTRUCTIONS

For the Cauliflower

1. Preheat the oven to 450°F.

2. Wash the cauliflower, then remove the green stems with a sharp knife. Trim the base so the cauliflower head can rest flat.

3. Place the cauliflower into a large baking dish or cast-iron skillet and pour the cup of water into the dish at the base.

4. In a small bowl, combine all the dried spices, along with the salt, black pepper, lemon juice, and 2 tablespoons (30 ml) of olive oil. Mix into a paste.

5. Using a silicone pastry brush or rubber spatula, spread the spice paste all over the head of cauliflower, working into the nooks and crannies.

6. Once coated, drizzle the top of the cauliflower with the 2 additional tablespoons of olive oil.

7. Cover the whole thing tightly with 1–2 pieces of aluminum foil, making sure to create a tight seal. We want to steam the cauliflower in the oven, prior to the finishing roast.

8. Place the baking dish into the oven and cook, covered, for 25 minutes.

9. After steaming for 25 minutes, uncover the cauliflower and roast for another 30 minutes, or until a knife slides easily into the center.

10. After cooking, remove the dish and let cool slightly on a wire rack.

11. Serve either in the pan, garnished with fresh parsley or cut individual slices, with the tahini sauce and honeyed cherries.

For the Cherries

1. Wash and dry the cherries. Using a cherry pitter, pit each fruit and add to a glass sealable jar.

2. Pour the olive oil, red wine vinegar, honey, cinnamon, and salt into the jar and close tightly.

3. Give the jar a firm couple of shakes and let marinate for at least 45 minutes. Periodically shake the container to move the juices.

4. Keeps refrigerated for up to a week.

For the Tahini Sauce

1. In a small mixing bowl, combine the tahini, lemon juice, olive oil, salt, and pepper. Fork-whisk. Fold in the chopped parsley.

2. Keep refrigerated for up to a week.

CRISPY SMASHED BABY POTATOES
WITH GARLIC, HERBS, AND FETA CHEESE · Serves 8 ·

These baby potatoes are cooked twice—first they are boiled until tender and then are smashed flat on a baking sheet before roasting with dill, garlic, and rosemary. They come out crispy and golden on the outside, but soft and creamy on the inside; we'll top these delicious bites with tangy crumbles of feta cheese to finish.

INGREDIENTS

1½ pounds (680 g) yellow baby potatoes

2 cups (475 ml) water

kosher salt

⅓ cup (80 ml) extra-virgin olive oil

3 cloves (15 g) garlic, crushed and minced

1 large (80 g) shallot, peeled and minced

2 sprigs fresh rosemary

¼ cup (2.5 g) packed fresh dill + more for garnish

freshly ground black pepper

3 tablespoons (25 g) feta crumbles

 Leave the feta cheese to the side and substitute dairy-free and vegan feta crumbles.

INSTRUCTIONS

1. Preheat the oven to 450°F and line a large baking sheet with parchment paper.

2. Quickly rinse the baby potatoes in a colander and add to a large pot. Add 2 cups (475 ml) water and a generous pinch of salt to the potatoes. Place over high heat and bring to a boil for 20–25 minutes, or until soft.

3. Remove from the water and spread the potatoes out on the baking sheet in one layer.

4. Using the bottom of a heavy drink glass or jam jar, gently squish the potatoes flat. The potatoes will flatten only while still quite warm, before the starches set.

5. In a small mixing bowl, add the olive oil, minced shallot, and minced garlic. Finely chop the leaves of 2 sprigs of rosemary, and the dill. Add to the bowl, then mix in a generous pinch of kosher salt and several grinds of black pepper. Stir well.

6. Using a spoon, dollop and spread the olive oil / herb mixture on top of each smashed potato.

7. Place the baking sheet in the oven and bake for 25 minutes, or until the potatoes are golden brown and crispy.

8. Remove from the oven and place the tray on a cooling rack.

9. Once mostly cooled, place the potatoes on a platter and top with feta cheese crumbles, and more fresh dill.

PUMPKIN PRETZEL BLONDIES
WITH CHOCOLATE CANDIES

We can't let this spooky holiday go without a super-fun dessert for all the ghosts and ghouls! Sweet pumpkin is incorporated into a classic blondie base, with hints of cinnamon, nutmeg, and brown sugar. We'll fold in colorful candy-coated chocolates and plenty of crunchy pretzels. This is a sweet treat— without any tricks!

INGREDIENTS

1 cup (120 g) light brown sugar

½ cup (100 g) white sugar

1 egg (about 55 g)

1 cup (245 g) pure pumpkin puree

1 teaspoon (4.8 g) vanilla extract

2 sticks (230 g) unsalted butter, melted

2¼ cups (290 g) all-purpose flour

1 teaspoon (4.5 g) baking powder

1 teaspoon (2.5 g) ground cinnamon

⅛ teaspoon (0.4 g) ground nutmeg

½ teaspoon (1.5 g) kosher salt

1 cup (100 g) mini pretzels + extra to garnish

1 cup (200 g) candy-coated chocolate candies
+ extra to garnish

INSTRUCTIONS

1. Preheat the oven to 350°F. Butter the bottom and sides of a 9-by-13-inch (22 × 33 cm) nonstick baking pan. Line with a sheet of parchment paper.

2. In the bowl of a stand mixer, beat together the light brown sugar, white sugar, vanilla extract, pumpkin puree, and egg on medium speed, until smooth.

3. Melt the two sticks of butter, either in a saucepan on the stove or in a nonmetallic bowl in the microwave. Let cool slightly, then slowly add the melted butter to the mixer bowl, mixing to completely incorporate.

4. In a medium-sized mixing bowl, add the flour, cinnamon, nutmeg, salt, and baking powder. Fork-stir. In small batches, add these dry ingredients to the wet ingredients, mixing until smooth.

5. Remove the bowl from the mixer stand. Stir in the pretzels and chocolate candies by hand, scraping down the sides of the bowl with a rubber spatula.

6. Pour the batter into the prepared pan and spread evenly. Smooth the tops with an offset spatula.

7. You can (optionally) drop extra pretzels or chocolate pieces on top of the batter and press them down slightly to embed them on top of the blondies.

8. Bake for 30–35 minutes, or until the middle has set and the edges are just pulling away from the pan.

9. Let the blondies cool in the pan on a cooling rack, until they reach room temperature. Remove from the pan, transfer to a large cutting board, and cut into squares. Store in a covered container.

THANKSGIVING FEAST

CRANBERRY APEROL SPRITZ

An autumn interpretation of a classic Italian aperitif! Aperol is stirred with sweet prosecco and a homemade spiced cranberry simple syrup. Topped with a splash of soda water and garnished with frozen cranberries. The cranberry simple syrup can be made up to a week in advance.

NEW ENGLAND–STYLE CRANBERRY SAUCE WITH ORANGE AND MAPLE SYRUP

A Thanksgiving must-have, my whole-berry cranberry sauce is flavored with cinnamon, orange, and pure maple syrup. A sweet and tart accompaniment to the holidays. This sauce can be made up to 3 days in advance.

SOURDOUGH BREAD STUFFING WITH TURKEY SAUSAGE AND CRANBERRIES

Crusty sourdough bread is broiled with sage, poultry seasoning, garlic, and butter until golden and toasty. It's mixed with a traditional combination of carrots, onions, and celery, and we'll up the "wow" factor with crumbled turkey sausage and dried cranberries. This recipe can be prepared the day before the event, but do not add the broth until immediately before cooking.

OVEN-ROASTED TURKEY WITH FRESH HERBS AND APPLES

Roasting a whole turkey is easier and faster than you think. We'll brine a bird in a homemade fall-themed brine and then roast at a high temperature for perfectly golden-brown skin and juicy meat.

APPLE AND PEAR CRUMBLE

All the flavors of a traditional apple pie, but a tenth of the work! Juicy apples and pears are baked under a traditional crumble of butter, flour, and sugar. The fruit melts and becomes syrupy, while the crumble brings out all that lovely pie crust flavor, without ever using a rolling pin!

CRANBERRY APEROL SPRITZ

• Makes one large wineglass •

The classic Aperol spritz is a refreshing Italian cocktail made with only 4 components: prosecco, simple syrup, soda water, and the orange-flavored aperitif Aperol. It's a festive and low-alcohol-to-volume drink that's perfect for your party! Here it's paired with a delightful cranberry-orange simple syrup, to match the festiveness of the holidays.

INGREDIENTS

4 ounces (120 ml) prosecco

2 ounces (60 ml) Aperol

1 ounce (30 ml) Cranberry Orange Simple Syrup (*see page 172*)

1 ounce (30 ml) soda water

optional garnishes:
frozen cranberries, orange slice, or edible flowers

INSTRUCTIONS

1. Take a large wineglass and fill halfway with ice.

2. Pour in the Aperol and simple syrup.

3. Next, add the prosecco and gently stir.

4. Finally, top off with soda water.

5. Garnish with an orange slice, frozen cranberries, or edible flowers like dianthus.

Cranberry Orange Simple Syrup

This easy-to-make simple syrup adds a tart sweetness to any cocktail. Using a bit of my New England–Style Cranberry Sauce, we'll infuse this lovely syrup with lots of sweet and tart notes!

• Makes about 1 cup •

INGREDIENTS

¼ cup (80 g) New England–Style Cranberry Sauce
(*see page 173*)

1 cup (200 g) sugar

1 cup (240 ml) water

zest of 1 navel orange (without the pith)

1 cinnamon stick

INSTRUCTIONS

6. Add all the ingredients to a small saucepan and mix.

7. Place the pot on medium-high heat and bring to a low boil for 5 minutes, stirring occasionally.

8. After boiling, remove from the heat and let cool slightly before straining into a glass mason jar with a fitted lid. Discard the solids.

9. Store covered in the refrigerator for up to 2 weeks.

NEW ENGLAND–STYLE CRANBERRY SAUCE WITH ORANGE AND MAPLE SYRUP

• Makes about 2 cups •

I'm from New England, and my love for the cranberry runs deep! Delicious maple syrup, orange juice, cinnamon, and whole fresh cranberries are boiled down to a sweet and refreshingly tart sauce. The cranberries "pop" under the heat and give this side dish that deep, beautiful, red-ruby color.

INGREDIENTS

12 ounces (340 g) whole fresh cranberries

¾ cup (180 g) real maple syrup
(amber/medium color)

½ cup (120 ml) water

½ cup (120 ml) orange juice, freshly squeezed,
or store bought

1 cinnamon stick

INSTRUCTIONS

1. Place cranberries into a large sieve. Discard any berries that look damaged (black spots, mushy, or very pale). Wash and drain.

2. Pour the cranberries into a medium-large pot. Add the maple syrup, water, and orange juice. Add a cinnamon stick and stir to combine.

3. Heat the berries on medium-high heat, until the mixture reaches a boil. Lower the heat to medium low and simmer for 10–12 minutes, or until syrupy and richly red (you will hear the cranberries "pop" as they cook!).

4. After 10–12 minutes, remove the pot from the heat and allow to cool to room temperature.

5. Store in a covered container in the fridge.

6. Serve at room temperature or slightly warmed.

173

SOURDOUGH BREAD STUFFING
WITH TURKEY SAUSAGE AND CRANBERRIES · Serves 8–10 ·

Stuffing can be as varied as the regions it's served in. From traditional oyster stuffing in New England to corn dressing from the South, what stays the same is the love put into it. I make my stuffing with toasted sourdough, savory sausage, and tangy dried cranberries, the ingredients and flavors of my childhood kitchen!

Note: For food safety I bake my stuffing outside the turkey. To bring back the extra flavor lost by not cooking stuffing inside the bird, I use a poultry bone broth to moisten the ingredients before baking.

INGREDIENTS

For the Bread Croutons

1 sourdough boule (slightly stale preferred!) (about 600 g)

¼ cup (60 g) butter, melted

2 teaspoons (7.5 g) garlic powder

2 teaspoons (1.5 g) dried parsley

2 tablespoons (30 ml) olive oil

3 teaspoons (6 g) Bell's Seasoning
(this is a poultry seasoning containing rosemary, oregano, sage, ginger, marjoram, thyme, and pepper)

pinch (1.2 g) kosher salt

freshly ground pepper

For the Stuffing

3 stalks (180 g) celery, trimmed

2 large (250 g) carrots, peeled

1 medium (160 g) yellow onion, peeled

16 ounces (450 g) turkey breakfast sausage (uncooked)

2 cloves (10 g) fresh garlic

1 tablespoon (5 g) fresh sage, chopped

4 sprigs (0.5 g) fresh thyme leaves, stems removed

1 spring fresh rosemary, stems removed

1 cup (160 g) dried unsweetened cranberries

½–1 cup (120–240 ml) chicken bone broth or rich turkey stock

1 tablespoon (15 ml) olive oil

kosher salt

freshly ground black pepper

INSTRUCTIONS

To Make the Bread Croutons

1. Preheat the oven to 375°F and reserve a large baking tray.

2. Slice and cube your bread into 1-inch (5 cm) cubes or hand-tear the bread into bite-sized pieces. Add to a large mixing bowl.

3. Melt the butter and mix with the olive oil, then add to the bread. Toss to coat.

4. Sprinkle on the Bell's seasoning and a generous pinch of kosher salt and pepper. Again, toss to coat.

5. Spread the bread in a single layer on the large baking tray and place into the oven for 10 minutes.

6. After 10 minutes, flip the bread cubes over and bake for an additional 10 minutes.

7. Let cool.

To Make the Stuffing

1. Dice the celery, carrots, and onion. Mince the garlic cloves and destem your herbs.

2. Set a large frying pan on high heat and add the turkey sausage. As the sausages cook, break them up into a crumble.

3. After fully cooking, set aside in a bowl but keep the drippings in the pan.

4. In the same pan that you cooked the turkey sausages, add 1 tablespoon of olive oil and reheat to medium-high heat.

5. Once hot, add the vegetables, garlic, and herbs to the pan. Add a generous pinch of salt and cook.

6. Stirring often, cook the vegetables until slightly wilted, watching for overbrowning. About 5–7 minutes.

7. Next, add the dried cranberries and cooked sausage to the pan. Let cook for 3 minutes while stirring.

8. Remove the pan from the heat.

To Assemble

1. In a large bowl, mix together the toasted bread cubes and cooked ingredients. Stir well with a large wooden spoon.

2. Grease a large casserole dish and add the bread stuffing mixture. Spread into an even layer.

3. Pour your stock or bone broth over top, but don't mix again. It will spread out naturally (if you have made the dish earlier and refrigerated, let it return to room temperature before baking).

4. Bake in a 375°F oven for 25 minutes.

5. Remove from the oven to a cooling rack.

OVEN-ROASTED TURKEY
WITH FRESH HERBS AND APPLES

Brining the turkey before roasting truly makes all the difference. I like to start brining my turkey 1–2 days before Thanksgiving dinner, so it has plenty of time to marinate. The mix of salt, spices, and aromatics adds flavor to the meat, but it also helps create that golden crispy skin after roasting. A combination of fresh herbs, garlic, and apple cider (or apple juice) infuses flavor into the turkey, and the results are always amazing: juicy and tender, with just enough flavor to enhance the roasted turkey meat.

There are many ways to roast a turkey. I like to use a high, constant temperature, 400°F, on convection mode, and I use a meat thermometer with a continuous digital readout to make sure the temperature is increasing linearly. At this roasting temperature, you must take the turkey out of the oven below your desired cooking temperature. Because the outside is at such a high temperature, I have found that a 15° rise for a 17–19-pound bird is expected with this cooking style. That is, if you are going for 160°F at the core, remove it at 145°F, since the core will continue to cook out of the oven.

INGREDIENTS

For the Brine

12 cups (2,800 ml) water

4 cups (950 ml) plain apple cider or unsweetened apple juice

1 cup (200 g) coarse kosher salt

½ cup (60 g) brown sugar

2 heads garlic

6 sprigs fresh thyme

6 sprigs fresh rosemary

3 dried bay leaves

1 tablespoon (7 g) whole black peppercorns

1 teaspoon (5 g) red pepper flakes

½ teaspoon (0.4 g) dried sage

For the Roast

One brined turkey (we usually use an 18-pound [8 kg] turkey for 12 servings)

2–3 apples (to fill the bird cavity)

2–3 yellow onions (to fill the bird cavity)

special equipment:

3–5-gallon (11–19 L) stock pot

1 large bag of ice

1 large cooler (depending on the climate in which you live!)

1 or 2 meat thermometers

INSTRUCTIONS

1. In a large stock pot, combine all brining ingredients. Slice the garlic heads around the circumference before adding to the pot. Place over medium-high heat and boil until the salt and sugar have completely dissolved. Stir occasionally.

2. Once the salt and sugar have dissolved, remove from heat. Add the apple cider and mix. Let the brine come to room temperature and then chill in the refrigerator (or if you live in a colder climate, outside) until cold.

3. Once the brine is chilled, we can use it to brine the turkey. If your turkey is less than 18 pounds, it should fit in a 4- or 5-gallon (15–19 L) stockpot, and you can brine directly in the pot. Otherwise, you may need a brining bag and a large cooler.

4. Make sure your turkey is completely thawed, the neck and bag of gizzards removed, and that it has been thoroughly rinsed inside and outside.

5. Into your large stockpot or brining bag, scoop or pour the brining mix so it fills above the top of the turkey. Be sure the cavity of the turkey is not blocked at the bottom and is being filled as well.

6. After filling, cover the stockpot (or tie the top of the brining bag securely).

7. If you live in a cooler climate, and the outside temperature is in the 35°F–45°F (2°C–7°C) range, just put the turkey in the stockpot outside. If you live anywhere warmer, place the stockpot in the bottom of a cooler and fill the cooler around it with ice. If you live somewhere where the stockpot will freeze overnight, place it in your garage or somewhere that will stay at refrigeration temperatures. You can let the turkey brine for 24–48 hours.

8. When ready to roast, remove the turkey from the brine, rinse in the sink, and wipe dry with paper towels. Discard the brine.

For the Roast

1. Place your rinsed and dried turkey in a roasting pan and stuff the cavity with quartered onions and apples (this is not to eat, so you can keep the skins on the onions). The purpose is to occupy space inside the turkey to prevent drying out. The apples and onions block hot oven air from heating the inside of the bird, allowing it to cook more evenly.

2. Prop the turkey up on its wings, folding them under the back of the bird, so it looks as though it will rest on its "elbows." This will keep the rest of the meat far away from any juices that come out of the bird while cooking.

3. Coat the outside of your turkey with vegetable or avocado oil. I just pour some on the top and rub it around with my hands. This will help with browning. You can use a butter coating as well, but I have found that the high-temperature-safe oils brown the turkey beautifully.

4. Roast the turkey at 400°F until it reaches 15°F below your desired temperature. Cover the turkey with foil when you remove it from the oven, and keep the thermometer in to ensure the temperature reaches the final cooking point you are trying for.

5. Once you've reached your desired temperature, let stand at least 30 minutes, then slice and enjoy!

APPLE AND PEAR CRUMBLE

If comfort can be distilled into dessert form, this is it wrapped up in a buttery-sweet, warm apple-and-pear hug. Even before you taste the first spoonful, the air is perfumed with cinnamon, and the smell is of delicately baked fruits. The beauty of this classic autumn dessert is it has all of the amazing flavors of Grandma's Thanksgiving apple pie, but without the extra stress of making, rolling, and cutting the dough. Just add the apples and pears to a dish and cover with the sugared crumble. Bake and serve with a scoop of your favorite vanilla ice cream!

INGREDIENTS

4 large honeycrisp apples (about 800 g)

2 large Bartlett pears (about 500 g), washed

1 teaspoon (4.8 g) vanilla extract

¼ teaspoon (0.75 g) kosher salt

2 teaspoons (5 g) cornstarch

1 cup (128 g) all-purpose flour

1 cup (200 g) sugar

½ teaspoon (1.3 g) ground cinnamon

½ cup (115 g) cold butter, cubed

optional:
vanilla ice cream or whipped cream for serving

INSTRUCTIONS

1. Preheat the oven to 350°F and butter a 9-by-13-inch (23 × 33 cm) baking dish.

2. Peel and core your apples. Cut into quarters and then slice thinly (⅛ inch, or 25 cm). Add them to a large mixing bowl.

3. Next, cut the pear from the core in quarters, leaving the skin on. Slice into ⅛-inch (25 cm) slices. Add to the bowl of apples.

4. Sprinkle the apples and pears with the salt, vanilla, and cornstarch. Gently mix and set aside.

5. In another large mixing bowl, add the flour, sugar, and cinnamon. Mix quickly with a fork.

6. Add the butter, and—using your hands—incorporate the butter into the dry mix. "Squish" the butter in, using the heat from your hands to melt it slightly.

7. When the butter starts to clump with the flour, begin to crumble up the clumps. The end result should look like a mix of sandy dough, with a few larger chunks.

8. Add the sliced apples and pears to the prepared baking dish. Spread the fruit out to even thickness.

9. Spread the "sandy" crumble mixture all over the fruit.

10. Bake 40–50 minutes on the middle rack, until golden and slightly bubbly.

11. Let cool for at least 15 minutes before serving. (I like to let mine rest for about 40 minutes, so the crumble is still warm, but not too hot; that way I can top with a scoop of ice cream and not have it immediately melt!)

 Replace the dairy butter with equal amounts of vegan European-style plant-based butter. To make this recipe gluten-free as well, swap the all-purpose flour for *Bob's Red Mill Gluten Free 1-to-1 Baking Flour.*

THANKSGIVING FEAST

TABLESCAPE

Thanksgiving is my favorite holiday of the year, and it's the first of the "Big Three" in North America: Thanksgiving, Christmas, and New Year's. To make decorating easier, I like to focus on texture for this lovely scene! A bountiful floral centerpiece is created in an heirloom crystal bowl. Crystal wineglasses and antique floral bone china are placed on contrasting woven place mats. Bowls of fresh purple figs and grapes line the table. Tall pillar candlesticks and petite silver votives light the room. This tablescape is elegant, but inviting.

COLOR

We'll use a variety of seasonal colors, to create a multidimensional bouquet. I focused on deep purples, pinks, and reds, with yellow-green, green, and yellow varieties.

BLOOMS

roses, dahlias, hydrangea, silver dollar eucalyptus, statice flowers, Canterbury bells, bupleurum, and green thistle flower

THE DETAILS

Because texture is the name of the game for this table, I've used a patterned, quilted table runner with a white-and-blue pattern. Rustic wooden candlesticks contrast with delicate glass pillars. Cut-crystal wineglasses give a little sparkle to the table, as does the cut-crystal fruit bowl used as the floral vessel. Touches of gold, deep purples, and orange are spread across the table to add visual interest. Wooden fall decor in the form of carved pumpkins and gourds brings a fun fall touch.

WHAT YOU'LL NEED

a large crystal vessel or vase

assorted flowers and greens

wooden tall candlesticks

glass candlesticks

assorted pillar candles

textured place mats

dishware with delicate details

crystal wineglasses

white or neutral-colored napkins

gold-toned napkin rings

assorted small bowls and cheese boards

fresh fall produce, such as mission figs, grapes, and small gourds

small snacks such as candied nuts, chocolate, or hard cheeses

decorative objects, such as wooden pumpkins, marble carved fruit, or other organic-shaped items

Set the Table

Location

A large dining room or hall.

Order of Operations

For this tablescape, I started by draping a runner across the length of the table, then set the large floral arrangement in the center. Next, my various candlesticks and votives were placed in small groupings down the table runner, with decorative objects added to any blank spots. A small cheeseboard or cake stand holding chocolate, candied nuts, and fruits was added to the table for guests to have easy access to small bites. Place settings were prepared with a textured place mat, dinner plate, salad plate, and napkin (in a decorative napkin ring). Silverware, water, and wineglasses were set out last. With all of that done, it's time to light the candles and celebrate!

Small Touches

I've set out bowls of fresh fall fruits and candied nuts as well as scattered the remaining gourds and fruits in bunches of three to five, throughout the table. This helps provide not only interest to the table, but also a little snack to tide your guests over until the meal is served!

Winter

There's a special sparkle to winter holiday parties. They seem bigger and more colorful than all the others. Maybe it's an innate response to repel the white and dull-gray hues of the outdoor weather. Whatever the reason, it's our habit to try to crank up the vibrancy inside, where it's snug and warm.

I like to imagine the days being filled with sledding and snow forts, holiday songs and traditions, warming foods, and storytelling by the fireplace. Even as the garden sleeps and dreams of spring, we can find joy in gathering together during the short days and long nights of wintertime.

MENUS

CHANNUKAH NOSH PARTY

CREAMY MOCHA BOURBON COCKTAIL

A bourbon-based drink, with notes of chocolate, Kahlúa, and fresh espresso. Garnished with a gilded chocolate coin. The simple syrup can be made up to a week in advance.

CLASSIC POTATO LATKES WITH SWEET AND SAVORY GARNISHES

Crispy, crunchy, shredded potato and onion latkes, deep fried until golden brown. Topped with a choice of sauces: a savory lemon-sour cream, or a sweet cinnamon and cardamom apple-pear sauce. The sauces can be made the day before.

TRADITIONAL SLAVIC FRUIT COMPOTE

An ode to one of my family's classic dishes. A mixture of fresh and dried fruits, slowly stewed with a magical combination of sugar, cinnamon, and whole cloves. Deeply aromatic and full of winter memories. This dish can be made a week in advance, if needed.

HARVEST WALDORF SALAD

A combination of green grapes, apples, dried dates, and pecans, served on a bed of greens. (*See page 139.*)

DARK CHOCOLATE AND TAHINI BROWNIES WITH GELT

Dense and dark, these chocolate brownies are given the holiday treatment! An extra layer of sweet and nutty tahini batter is swirled on top, and then they're garnished with gold-brushed chocolate coins. The brownies can be made the day before, if desired.

CREAMY MOCHA BOURBON COCKTAIL

This is a cocktail that feels like sipping on a "grown-up" chocolate milk! The bite of bourbon mixed with espresso is tempered with Kahlúa, milk, and a dash of chocolate bitters. Smooth and sweet, this is a lovely mocha cocktail to help relieve the tension of eight crazy nights!

INGREDIENTS

2 ounces (60 ml) brewed espresso, preferably chilled

1½ ounces (45 ml) bourbon of your choice

1 ounce (30 ml) Kahlúa

1 ounce (30 ml) 2% milk

½ ounce (15 ml) simple syrup

dash of chocolate bitters

chocolate candy coins

gold-luster food coloring

ice

INSTRUCTIONS

1. Prepare a shot of espresso, then chill until needed.

2. Peel the foil wrappers from your gold chocolate coins. Add a few drops of gold food coloring to a coin, then gently rub with a paper towel to add some gleam. Repeat for the number of cocktails you'll be serving, and place the coins on a clean paper towel to dry until needed.

3. In the cup of a cocktail shaker add the bourbon, Kahlúa, milk, and simple syrup.

4. Next, add a large handful of ice and pour in the espresso.

5. Close the shaker and vigorously shake for 30 seconds, or until chilled.

6. Fill an Old-Fashioned glass with a scoop of ice.

7. Using a cocktail strainer, strain the cocktail into the prepared glass.

8. Garnish with a gold-burnished chocolate coin and enjoy!

CLASSIC POTATO LATKES
WITH SWEET AND SAVORY GARNISHES

• Serves 8–10 •

Is there really anything better than sinking your teeth into a crispy fried potato pancake with sour cream? Maybe only if it's topped with a delicious cooked-fruit compote! Here, golden-fried russet potato pancakes are topped with two homemade sauces that will make you keep coming back for more. I like to prepare these sauces in advance to let the flavors meld, but I totally understand jumping right in and enjoying these crispy latkes all by themselves!

 Replace the traditional dairy sour cream with your favorite almond milk or cashew milk plant-based sour cream.

INGREDIENTS

6 large russet potatoes (about 1,700 g), washed and peeled

1 medium yellow onion (about 170 g), peeled

4 tablespoons (48 g) potato starch

1 tablespoon (9 g) kosher salt

freshly ground black pepper

2 eggs (about 110 g)

vegetable or avocado oil for pan frying

plenty of paper towels!

INSTRUCTIONS

I personally prefer to fry latkes in a large cast-iron pan, which is excellent at retaining heat when you add in the cold potato, but any large skillet can do the job!

1. Working in batches, use a box grater or a food processor with grating attachment to shred the peeled potatoes. Add to a large mixing bowl.

2. Cut the peeled yellow onion into quarters, then grate using the food processor (or box grater). Combine with the potatoes in large mixing bowl.

3. To the large bowl, add the salt, black pepper, and potato starch.

4. Place a large mesh strainer or sieve over the sink and transfer the grated vegetables into it, pressing firmly down, to release any extra water. This may take several rounds, but try to squeeze as much liquid out as you can before returning the grated vegetables to the large bowl. This moisture-reducing step helps the texture of the latkes and reduces splatter when you place them to cook.

5. Place a large pan over medium-high heat.

6. In a small bowl, whisk two eggs and then add the mixture to the onion/potato blend.

7. Mix thoroughly with your hands.

8. Prepare a large plate with several paper towels, to absorb excess oil.

9. Add ¼ cup (60 ml) of vegetable or avocado oil to your skillet and let heat. Be careful, since it will quickly become extremely hot!

10. Take about ¼ cup (about 60 g) of the potato mixture in your hands, squeeze any additional moisture out, then add carefully to the hot oil. Using a spoon, spread the potatoes by pressing down. I usually size to fit 3–4 potato pancakes per 12-inch (30 cm) skillet.

11. Let fry for 4–5 minutes on each side. They should get crispy.

12. After the latkes are golden brown, place on a plate with paper towels underneath to drain off excess oil. Add another layer of paper towels if you want to stack a second batch on top of the first.

13. Repeat the process, adding more oil as needed to ensure even frying.

14. For reheating, place the latkes on a baking sheet in the oven and heat at 350°F for 10 minutes.

Dried Lemon and Fresh Chive Sour Cream Sauce

· Makes about 1 cup (240 ml) ·

INGREDIENTS

3 tablespoons (15 g) minced fresh green chives

1 cup (240 g) regular sour cream

¼ teaspoon (0.6 g) dried lemon peel (substitute ½ teaspoon [1.2 g] fresh lemon zest if needed)

generous pinch (1.8 g) kosher salt

freshly ground black pepper to taste

INSTRUCTIONS

1. In a small mixing bowl, add all the ingredients and stir well.

2. Adjust the salt and pepper to taste.

3. Cover and refrigerate until serving.

Apple-Pear Sauce with Green Cardamom and Cinnamon

• Makes about 1½ cups (350 ml) •

INGREDIENTS

2 (about 400 g) large gala apples, peeled

2 (about 500 g) Bartlett pears, skin on

½ lemon, juiced (1 5ml juice)

½ cup (100 g) sugar

½ teaspoon (1.3 g) ground cinnamon

3 green cardamom pods, cracked

splash of water

INSTRUCTIONS

1. Roughly chop the pears and peeled apples.

2. Add to a medium saucepan, along with the lemon juice, sugar, cinnamon, and cracked green cardamom pods.

3. Add a splash of water and place on medium-high heat.

4. Cook for 20–25 minutes, stirring occasionally, until soft and mushy.

5. Remove from the heat and discard the cardamom pods.

6. Using a potato masher, mash the fruit to release any juices.

7. Transfer to a covered container and chill.

8. Allow to come to room temperature for about 30 minutes before serving.

This is also a wonderful dessert topping, yogurt add-in, or pastry filling.

TRADITIONAL SLAVIC FRUIT COMPOTE

• Makes about 2 cups (475 ml) •

This is one of those flavor profiles that triggers a flood of memories for me. My mum would make variations of this compote for special occasions, religious holidays, and even Thanksgiving! The recipe was found in the depths of my mum's recipe box, written in my great-grandmother's spindly script on the back of an old envelope. This sweet and fragrant stewed-fruit dish tastes like home. A combination of dried apricots, cherries, and prunes are mixed with fresh apples and pears. The Old World trifecta of cloves, cinnamon, and sugar will scent your house and announce in more than mere words that it is indeed the holidays!

INGREDIENTS

½ cup (80 g) dried prunes

½ cup (60 g) dried apricots

½ cup (80 g) dried cherries

½ cup (100 g) sugar

½ cup (120 ml) water

1 lemon, juiced (30 ml juice)

4 whole cloves

1 cinnamon stick

1 large (200 g) firm-fleshed apple
(like gala or Cortland), peeled

2 (500 g) Bartlett pears

INSTRUCTIONS

1. Using a medium pot, add the dried fruits, sugar, lemon juice, water, and spices.

2. With a sharp knife, cut the fruit from the core of the apple and pear and slice into ⅛-inch-thick (25 cm) slices. Add to the pot.

3. Place the pot over medium-high heat and bring to a boil. Stir occasionally.

4. Once at a boil, lower the heat to a simmer and let it cook for about 30 minutes, until the dried fruits are plump and the fresh fruits are stewed and soft. Add a splash of water if the liquid boils off.

5. After cooking, let cool for 10 minutes, then discard the cinnamon stick and cloves.

6. Transfer to a covered container and chill.

7. Bring to room temperature before serving.

DARK CHOCOLATE AND TAHINI BROWNIES WITH GELT • Makes 12 squares •

I love a good brownie to end a meal! Chewy on the edges, but decadently dense on the inside, these dark chocolate treats are elevated with a sesame tahini swirl, giving them a subtle layer of nuttiness. We'll make them Channukah-ready with some festively gilded chocolate coins.

INGREDIENTS

8 ounces (225 g) high-quality baking chocolate, 60% cacao

1 stick (115 g) unsalted butter + more for greasing the pan

3 tablespoons (15 g) high-quality cocoa powder

3 eggs (about 165 g)

1¼ cups (250 g) sugar

1 teaspoon (4.8 g) vanilla extract

½ teaspoon (1.5 g) + 1 small pinch (1 g) kosher salt, separated

1 cup (128 g) all-purpose flour

2 tablespoons (30 g) tahini paste

12–16 candy chocolate coins, peeled

gold-gilt food-coloring gel

INSTRUCTIONS

1. Preheat the oven to 350°F and prepare a 9-by-9-inch (23 × 23 cm) baking pan with a sheet of parchment to fit the bottom. Butter the sides of the pan. Reserve.

2. Break the baking chocolate into chunks and cut the butter into pieces. Melt together the butter and chocolate, either in a double boiler or (in a nonmetallic bowl) in the microwave in 30-second increments, stirring in between sessions. Heat until smooth and creamy.

3. In a large bowl, whisk together the eggs, sugar, vanilla extract, and salt.

4. Place ⅓ cup (80 ml) of this mixture in a separate bowl, add the tahini and 1 tablespoon (8 g) of flour, and stir to combine. This will be the "tahini batter."

5. To the larger bowl of batter, add the melted chocolate and butter, stirring with a rubber spatula or large wooden spoon to combine. This will be the "chocolate batter."

6. Add the rest of the flour to the chocolate batter and stir well.

7. Pour the chocolate batter into the prepared pan and spread with an offset spatula to smooth.

8. Using a spoon, dollop the tahini batter on top of the chocolate batter. Take a spoon, or long skewer, and slightly mix the two batters to create a marbling effect.

9. Bake in the oven on the middle rack at 350°F for 30–35 minutes, or until a toothpick comes out cleanly from the center.

10. Remove from the oven and place on a wire cooling rack.

11. Using a paper towel, add a few drops of gold food coloring and then rub onto the front of the peeled chocolate coins.

12. After the brownies have cooled for about 10 minutes, sink chocolate coins, evenly spaced, halfway into the top. The coins will soften slightly.

13. Let the brownies cool completely, then remove from the pan.

14. Cut into squares and plate, or store in a covered container until use.

 Replace the all-purpose flour with *Bob's Red Mill Gluten Free 1-to-1 Baking Flour* and be sure to use a gluten-free brand of sesame tahini.

CHANNUKAH NOSH PARTY

TABLESCAPE

Channukah is known as the festival of light. Traditionally celebrated in the early winter, this holiday encourages people to eat foods fried in oil, play with dreidels, and enjoy loads of sweets! I have created this party as a multiappetizer meal, rather than a sit-down dinner. For the tablescape, the focus will be on the flowers and candlelight.

COLOR

For this Channukah table, we're working with a complementary color palette of blue and yellow orange. We'll bring added brightness and depth with touches of white and blue violet.

BLOOMS

roses, purple lisianthus, aster, Queen Anne's lace, and stalks of millet

THE DETAILS

Light-green textured glass goblets and pink accent linens set the scene. Woven basket-weave place mats and neutral-colored dishware help highlight the bright palette of pastels and make the flowers pop off the table. Tall crystal and wooden candlesticks are used to hold hand-rolled beeswax pillars. Small ornamental touches are scattered around the table, including a pair of charming ceramic fox and rabbit vases, as well as several hand-blown eggshells, used as delicate flower vessels. Giant hosta leaves serve as a burst of vernal color at each setting. A large decorative vase in the shape of a classic Roman bust takes center stage, with a "crown" of heavy peonies and delicate irises.

WHAT YOU'LL NEED

1 large silvered glass compote bowl vase

assorted flowers and greens

1–2 table runners in shades of blue

blue-and-white cloth napkins

blue-and-white patterned dishware

3 blue-glass pillar candleholders

4 amber-colored-glass votive holders

beeswax pillars and votives

dreidels

gelt (chocolate coins)

assorted heirlooms

Set the Table

Location

A dining room or living room.

Order of Operations

Drape your table runners across the length of your surface. If they are long enough, gently bunch to create a "flowing water" effect. Place your large flower arrangement toward the center of the table. Next, add your glass pillar candlesticks and votives in small groupings, along with a scattering of gold coins and wooden dreidels. Add your menorah, as well as stacked service dishware for guests who want to collect a few bites at a time. Place napkins by the dishware or on a side table where you serve drinks.

Small Touches

I've added several pieces of new and vintage Judaica to the scene. Celebrations are just as much about family as they are about a beautiful table, so adding something personal can have a lot of meaning!

CHRISTMAS MORNING BRUNCH

PEPPERMINT WHITE HOT CHOCOLATE

A creamy white-chocolate hot cocoa, flavored with peppermint extract and topped with whipped cream and crushed peppermints. This recipe is wonderful by the cup, or you can batch it and set up a hot-chocolate bar for a DIY experience!

APPLE CHAI SOURDOUGH SCONES

A delicious treat filled with fragrant chai and juicy apples. Flaky and tender, and the added sourdough starter scrap adds a tasty tang to these classic pastries. These scones can be made the day before.

GIANT GINGERBREAD CINNAMON ROLL WITH ESPRESSO ICING

Can we say showstopper? Combining two holiday favorites, this giant sweetbread cinnamon roll is filled with traditional gingerbread spices, brown sugar, and butter. Topped with an espresso icing. The rolls can be made the day before, but not baked until the day of.

ASPARAGUS AND SMOKED GOUDA CRUSTLESS QUICHE

This quiche is a hearty protein-and-veggie fix to balance an otherwise sweet Christmas morning! It can be made the day before and reheated. See page 57.

LEMON TART WITH PECAN GRAHAM CRACKER CRUST

A sunny fresh lemon tart is always welcome on a holiday dessert table! Silky smooth lemon curd meets a crunchy sweet pecan and graham cracker crust. Topped with fresh raspberries and whipped cream. This tart can be made the day before, but the raspberries and whipped cream should be fresh.

PEPPERMINT WHITE HOT CHOCOLATE • Makes 4–6 servings •

A coffee-house-style classic that you can easily enjoy at home, this version of peppermint hot chocolate is a yummy treat for adults and kids alike! In case you're trying to make this delicious drink even more "adult," you could easily add a splash of chocolate liqueur!

INGREDIENTS

4 cups (950 ml) 2% milk

1 cup (160 g) premium white-chocolate chips / morsels

1 teaspoon (4.8 g) vanilla extract

¼ teaspoon (1.2 g) peppermint extract

peppermint candies and whipped cream for garnish

INSTRUCTIONS

1. In a large pot, add the milk and place over medium heat. Stir occasionally. Be careful not to scald the milk: heat until just steaming, then remove from the heat.

2. Add the white-chocolate chips, vanilla extract, and peppermint extract to the hot milk. Stir with a rubber spatula or wire whisk until the chocolate has completely melted into the milk.

3. Ladle the peppermint white hot chocolate into your favorite mugs. Garnish with whipped cream and crushed peppermint candies.

Replace the dairy milk with your favorite plant-based milk (I prefer a coconut/cashew milk blend). Choose a gluten-free vegan white-chocolate-chip brand and follow the directions as written. I love some of the ready-made coconut whip in the grocery store as a topping, and it's convenient too.

APPLE CHAI SOURDOUGH SCONES

• Makes 12 •

I fell in love with the science of sourdough starter several years ago. Besides making delicious breads, you can use the scrap to bake these award-winning pastries too! These scones are tender and flaky, and just bursting with the flavor of apple and chai spice. I absolutely love them!

INGREDIENTS

3 cups (384 g) all-purpose flour

1 tablespoon (4.5 g) high-quality chai, ground finely in a mortar and pestle (or spice grinder)

1 cup (200 g) sugar

2 teaspoons (9 g) baking powder

½ teaspoon (1.3 g) ground cinnamon

½ teaspoon (1.5 g) salt

1 cup (275 g) sourdough starter, after peaking

¼ cup (60 ml) buttermilk or heavy cream

1 teaspoon (4.8 g) vanilla extract

1 egg (about 55 g)

1 cup (230 g) salted butter, cold and cubed

1 large (about 200 g) firm apple peeled, cored, and roughly cubed into ¼-inch (5 mm) pieces

¼ cup (50 g) raw sugar for sprinkling, optional

INSTRUCTIONS

1. Preheat the oven to 350°F and line two baking sheets with parchment paper.

2. In the bowl of a stand mixer, combine the flour, ground chai, sugar, ground cinnamon, baking powder, and salt. Mix lightly to combine.

3. In a separate medium-sized mixing bowl, combine the sourdough starter, buttermilk (or heavy cream), vanilla extract, and 1 egg. Hand-whisk to combine. Rest for 5–7 minutes.

4. On low speed, add the cold butter one cube at a time into the bowl of the stand mixer with the dry ingredients. Do this slowly and on a low speed to make sure the butter is mixed throughout. About 7 minutes.

5. With the mixer speed on medium low, carefully add the wet mixture to the dry ingredients, until just combined. Stop the mixer and stir in the apple cubes.

6. The dough will seem a little dry, and this is correct (you don't want a fully incorporated dough, or it won't end up with the more crumbly texture of a scone).

7. Turn out the "crumbly" dough to a lightly floured cutting board or floured countertop.

8. Using your hands with as little kneading as possible, bring the dough together into a loose rectangle. The heat of your hands will melt the butter a bit.

9. Press and shape as you bring the dough together. Try to get a flat dough about ¾–1 inch (2–2.5 cm) thick.

10. Using a sharp cutting knife, slice into 12 more or less square pieces.

11. Using a spatula, gently transfer the scones to the prepared cookie sheets. Leave space between each pastry to bake.

12. Sprinkle the tops of the scones with raw sugar (optional).

13. Bake for 25 minutes, or until the bottom edges are golden brown and the tops are just starting to color.

14. Remove from the oven to a cooling rack. Let stand on the cookie sheets for 5 minutes and then transfer off the cookie sheet to a cooling rack. Let cool completely.

15. Cut each square diagonally, for a traditional "scone" triangular shape.

GIANT GINGERBREAD CINNAMON ROLL WITH ESPRESSO ICING · Serves 8–10 ·

There is nothing like the scent of cinnamon rolls baking in the oven on a cold winter's day! To pull out all the stops for this special treat, a mixture of cinnamon and cloves are combined with the more traditional butter and brown sugar, making a far more fragrant filling. On top of everything is poured a rich espresso icing. Rather than making small individual buns, I like the look of one large roll that's perfect for slicing.

INGREDIENTS

For the Tangzhong Starter

5 tablespoons (75 ml) water

5 tablespoons (75 ml) whole milk

3 tablespoons + 1 teaspoon (27 g) all-purpose flour

For the Dough

4 cups (512 g) + 2 tablespoons (16 g) all-purpose flour

¼ cup (50 g) sugar

1¾ teaspoons (5.3 g) kosher salt

1 tablespoon (11 g) instant yeast

¼ cup (23 g) nonfat dry milk powder

¾ cup (180 ml) whole milk, warmed

2 large (110 g in total) eggs, room temperature

6 tablespoons (85 g) butter, melted

1 teaspoon (5 ml) vegetable oil

For the Gingerbread Filling

1 cup (120 g) dark brown sugar

1 tablespoon + 1 teaspoon (10 g) ground cinnamon

1 teaspoon (2.8 g) ground ginger

⅛ teaspoon (0.4 g) ground cloves

optional: ⅛ teaspoon (0.4 g) freshly ground nutmeg

5 tablespoons (70 g) butter, room temperature
(this is spread between the dough and the gingerbread spices during assembly)

For the Espresso Icing

1 cup (128 g) confectioners' sugar

2 tablespoons (28 g) butter, melted

1 shot of espresso (30 ml)

1 tablespoon (15 ml) whole milk

1 tablespoon (15 ml) half-and-half or light cream

½ teaspoon (2.4 g) vanilla extract

pinch (1.2 g) salt

special equipment:
1 9-inch (23 cm) springform pan

INSTRUCTIONS

To Make the Starter and Dough

1. In a saucepan, combine the 5 tablespoons (75 ml) of water, 5 tablespoons (75 ml) of whole milk, and 3 tablespoons + 1 teaspoon (27 g) of flour. Whisk to combine.

2. Place on medium-high heat and continue whisking until thickened into a paste (about 5 minutes), being careful

not to brown the paste. Remove from the heat. This is the "tangzhong starter."

3. Using the dough hook attachment, combine the additional flour, white sugar, salt, dry milk powder, instant yeast, warmed milk, melted butter, and eggs in the bowl of the stand mixer. Add the finished tangzhong starter into the mixer bowl as well.

4. Now, on medium speed, mix for about 3 minutes, or until a rough dough is formed.

5. Stop the mixer and remove any dough sticking to the hook. Cover the mixing bowl with a tea towel and place the bowl somewhere warm to rest for 20–25 minutes.

6. After resting, place the bowl and the dough hook back on the stand mixer.

7. Knead the dough on medium speed with the dough hook for about 2 minutes, until the dough is smooth and creates a tidy ball.

8. Taking a large, clean mixing bowl, lightly grease with the vegetable oil. Place the dough into the oiled bowl and then cover with a tea towel.

9. Let the dough rise for about 60 minutes in a warm environment, until it has doubled in size. The dough should be puffy, and when pressed with a finger, a dent should remain.

For the Gingerbread Filling

In a small mixing bowl, combine the brown sugar and all the spices and fork-mix.

To Assemble

1. Line the springform pan with a circle of parchment paper.

2. On a large, floured cutting board or countertop, turn out your dough. Using a lightly floured rolling pin, gently roll the dough out into a large rectangle (about the size of a baking sheet).

3. With an offset palate knife or butter knife, spread the room-temperature butter evenly over the rolled dough.

4. Take the gingerbread spice mixture and spread evenly over the butter, keeping a ½-inch (1 cm) border clear around the edges of the dough.

5. Using a sharp knife or pizza cutter, slice 4 strips lengthwise (if you are making one large cinnamon roll), or 8–10 thinner strips (if you are making individual rolls).

6. To roll as one large bun: take one of the lengthwise strips and firmly roll up over itself, trying to keep the edges even. After you've rolled the first strip, carefully lift and place the rolled dough at the start of the next strip. Continue to roll, while winding up around itself. Repeat the process until all the strips have been used.

7. Place the giant roll into a springform pan (I like to flip the roll upside down when placing, for a cleaner edge).

8. Gather up any filling that may have spilled out during the rolling process, and sprinkle on top.

9. Place a tea towel over the pan and let sit somewhere warm for about 60 minutes, for a final rise before baking.

To Bake

1. Preheat the oven to 350°F and prepare the middle rack for baking.

2. Take the cinnamon roll and bake in the oven for 25 minutes, or until golden brown.

3. Remove from the oven and let cool slightly on a cooling rack.

To Make the Icing

1. Using a medium-sized mixing bowl, whisk together the confectioners' sugar, salt, melted butter, espresso, milk, and vanilla extract.

2. Mix until smooth, about 1–2 minutes.

To Finish

1. Remove the roll from the springform pan and place on a large plate or platter.

2. Drizzle the icing evenly on top.

3. Serve warm.

LEMON TART
WITH PECAN GRAHAM CRACKER CRUST

There isn't any dessert quite like homemade lemon curd. Sweet, tart, and lively yellow in color, this dessert is delicious and surprisingly easy to make. A cheerful, yummy dessert for a Christmas brunch!

INGREDIENTS

For the Crust

1 individual package (8 crackers, or 120 g) plain graham crackers

1½ cups (100 g) vanilla wafer cookies

½ cup (60 g) raw pecans

6 tablespoons (85 g) butter, melted

generous pinch (1.8 g) kosher salt

For the Lemon Curd

½ cup (100 g) + ¼ cup (50 g) sugar, divided

½ cup freshly squeezed lemon juice (120 ml juice, or about 4 lemons)

1 tablespoon (10 g) fresh lemon zest

3 eggs (about 165 g), room temperature

¾ cup (170 g) butter, at room temperature

INSTRUCTIONS

For the Crust

1. Preheat the oven to 350°F. Reserve a 9-inch (23 cm) tart or pie plate.

2. Add the graham crackers and vanilla wafer cookies to the bowl of a food processor with the dough blade. Pulse several times until the mixture reaches a fairly fine crumb with some remaining texture. If a food processor isn't available, you can also crush by hand. Place crumb mixture in a large bowl.

3. Separately, place your pecans in the food processor and pulse until finely crushed. This is done without the other elements to allow more control over the processor and prevent accidentally making "peanut butter" rather than a fine grind.

4. Melt the 6 tablespoons of butter and add the salt, either in a pan on the stovetop or in a nonmetallic bowl in the microwave (stirring every 30 seconds).

5. Pour the butter on top of the crumb mixture and stir with a fork until incorporated. The crust will resemble crumbly wet sand.

6. Transfer the cookie crumb mixture into the center of your 9-inch (23 cm) pie or tart pan.

7. Gently push the crumbs to spread out in an even layer around the pan with your fingertips, or by rolling with a small drinking glass. Press the crumbs up the sides of the pan (about ¾ of the way to the edge).

8. Blind-bake (bake without filling) in the oven for 10–12 minutes, or until slightly browned.

9. Remove from the oven and let cool on a baking rack (make sure the crust cools completely before filling).

For the Lemon Curd

1. In a medium saucepan, add the lemon juice, lemon zest, and ½ cup (100g) of sugar, whisking to combine. Set over medium heat and bring to a boil, whisking occasionally. This will create a lemon syrup.

2. Once the syrup reaches a low boil remove from the heat.

3. In a medium mixing bowl, whisk the eggs and the ¼ cup (50 g) of sugar until combined. The eggs and sugar should be completely incorporated and almost smooth in texture.

4. To temper the egg mixture: Using a ladle, slowly pour a thin stream of the still-hot lemon syrup into the egg mixture, while whisking continuously. This action will warm the eggs slowly and avoid any scrambled egg curds.

5. Continue to pour in the lemon syrup in a thin stream, whisking continuously, until ⅓ of the simple syrup is incorporated.

6. After combining ⅓ of the syrup into the egg mixture, pour the entire bowl back into the medium saucepan, fully combining the lemon syrup with the eggs and sugar. Bring to a slow boil on medium heat while whisking. The liquid will begin to thicken after about 8 minutes.

7. After you've reached a low bubbling boil, continue whisking for an additional 1 minute. The curd will begin to look like a viscous hollandaise sauce.

8. Remove from the heat and let cool for 1 minute.

9. Slowly add the butter 1 chunk at a time, using a spatula to stir gently until each chunk is completely melted and incorporated.

To Assemble

1. Pour the slightly cooled lemon curd into the cooled tart shell. Cover with plastic wrap and refrigerate for at least 90 minutes (best overnight).

2. This dish is best served chilled.

3. Garnish with whipped cream and fresh red raspberries.

CHRISTMAS MORNING BRUNCH

TABLESCAPE

Santa has flown back to the North Pole, the presents under the tree have been opened by many excited hands, and a moment of calm settles over your household—it's time to celebrate! My Christmas table is filled with red, green, and white. Let's have a meal that your holiday guests will delight in!

COLOR

A traditional holiday color palette of red and green is a quintessential complementary color scheme. We'll add touches of gold, silver, and white to bring a wintry feel to our Christmas brunch.

BLOOMS

red and white roses, Queen Anne's lace, pine cones, and textured green filler

THE DETAILS

Beautiful Christmas-themed plates are topped with red and gold "bows"—napkins folded to resemble gift wrapping! Sparkling crystal Christmas trees glint in the candlelight, while small porcelain houses sit in imaginary snow. Pine cones are scattered across the table, and gift tags act as place cards.

WHAT YOU'LL NEED

1 medium-sized white urn-shaped vase

3 small jam jars

assorted flowers and grasses

decorative pine cones

1 gold- or silver-toned table runner

red- and gold-toned brocade napkins

gold-toned napkin, rings

gold- or silver-colored chargers

basket-woven place mats

Christmas-themed dishware

crystal wineglasses and water glasses

3 crystal Christmas trees of various heights, or crystal decorative elements

4–6 silver- and gold-colored glass votive holders with white votive candles

white or gold-toned decorative elements, such as Christmas houses, Christmas ornaments, or reindeer

artificial snow

card stock gift tags

Christmas tree stamp

ink pad for stamps

Set the Table

Location

A dining room or large hall.

Order of Operations

First, place the runner down the length of the table, then set the large floral arrangement in the center, and the smaller floral jars near the sides. Next are the main decorative foci. I like to use tall crystal elements (in this case, shaped like modernist Christmas trees) around the main centerpiece. Farther down the runner, my shorter elements, the silver votives, pine cone bunches, and small ceramic houses, surrounded by artificial snow.

After the principal decorations are complete, I add the table settings, starting with the place mat, chargers, dinner plates, and salad plates. Napkins are folded into a rectangle, then slid through the napkin ring and placed horizontally on the lower third of the salad plate, so it resembles a bow. Crystal and silverware are added last.

Small Touches

Using a Christmas tree stamp from my local craft store, I made cute individual holiday place cards for my guests. Simply press the stamp into the ink pad, then stamp several of the card stock gift tags. Write the names of your guests on each card and attach to a pine cone with a piece of twine. Arrange the pine cone with a tag on top of each plate.

NEW YEAR'S EVE COCKTAIL PARTY

HOLIDAY CHERRY GIN SOUR
WITH ROSEMARY SIMPLE SYRUP

A bright-red cherry twist to a classic gin sour! With hints of fresh rosemary, lime, and elderflower, this ethereal cocktail is garnished with brightly colored dried edible flowers. The simple syrup can be made up to a week in advance.

CRANBERRY APEROL SPRITZ

Need a backup cocktail option? This Aperol spritz can throw down in the winter as well! See page 171.

THAI-INSPIRED ROASTED CARROT
AND COCONUT MILK SOUP WITH LIME

A velvety-smooth soup that will absolutely bring everyone back for more. A complex and aromatic vegetable-heavy base that is perfectly spiced, with a wonderful balance of sweet and savory. This soup can be made the day before your event.

SEARED AHI TUNA WITH LIME AND HERB
GREMOLATA, GREEN GRAPES,
AND HONEY-LIME VINAIGRETTE

This tuna makes a great appetizer for any guest who wants a lighter alternative to the beef dish. The vinaigrette can be made the day before and paired with the tuna right before the event. See page 108.

SEARED BEEF CROSTINI WITH
WASABI MAYONNAISE AND MARINATED
CHERRY TOMATOES

This is a savory appetizer with lots of big, bold flavors. Thinly sliced steak, a hit of acid, and a punch of heat, all packaged on a crunchy slice of toast. You'll want to set some aside for yourself before they all disappear off the table!

PORT WINE SABAYON WITH FRESH BERRIES

A classic Italian dessert with a Portuguese twist! Simply made but beautifully presented, this "light as a feather" dessert custard is served over fresh sweet berries. This is a stress-free recipe for a delicious dessert, and an impressive way to present a bowl of fresh berries.

HOLIDAY CHERRY GIN SOUR
WITH ROSEMARY SIMPLE SYRUP • Makes one 6-ounce drink •

This is a drink that puts you in the "cocktail connoisseur" level of home mixology, layering together the flavors of sweet cherry with the herbaceousness of rosemary, floral notes of elderflower liqueur, and acidity of lime juice. A gin sour like this one definitely calls for a fresh egg-white-foam topper, but if that's not to your taste, you can substitute a tablespoon of vegan-friendly aquafaba instead. Visual pizzazz is added with colorful dried, edible flowers.

INGREDIENTS

2½ ounces (75 ml) gin with herbaceous notes
(such as Hendrick's)

1 ounce (30 ml) fresh lime juice

1 ounce (30 ml) unsweetened natural cherry juice

1 ounce (30 ml) Rosemary Simple Syrup (*see page 212*)

½ ounce (15m l) elderflower liqueur

1 fresh egg, or 1 ounce (30 ml) aquafaba

ice

fresh rosemary

for garnish:
fresh rosemary, freeze-dried edible flower petals, frozen
blackberries, or cherries

INSTRUCTIONS

1. In the cup of a cocktail shaker, add the tip needles of a fresh rosemary sprig and lime juice. Muddle together, using a cocktail muddler or the handle end of a large wooden spoon.

2. If using an egg, separate the egg white from the egg yolk. You need only the egg white (you can discard the yolk or use it for something like the Port Wine Sabayon on page 216).

3. Add the rest of the liquids to the shaker.

4. Scoop a large handful of ice into the shaker cup and add the fresh egg white (or aquafaba).

5. Close the cocktail shaker and shake vigorously for at least 30 seconds. Reserve.

6. Using a chilled coupe glass, run a leaf of fresh rosemary along the lip for scent.

7. Take a cocktail strainer and strain the drink into the coupe.

8. Garnish with freeze-dried edible flower petals, or a sprig of fresh rosemary.

Rosemary Simple Syrup

A basic cocktail syrup, infused with oils from the sprigs of fresh rosemary.

• Makes 1 cup (about 250 ml) •

INGREDIENTS

1 cup (200 g) sugar

1 cup (240 ml) water

2 large fresh rosemary sprigs

INSTRUCTIONS

1. In a medium-sized saucepan, combine the ingredients and stir lightly.

2. Place over medium-high heat and bring to a boil.

3. Let boil for 5 minutes and then remove from the heat. All sugar should be dissolved.

4. Let cool for 3 minutes and then strain into a glass jar with a tightly fitted lid. Discard the solids.

5. Chill in the refrigerator until use.

6. This syrup will stay for up to 2 weeks in the refrigerator.

THAI-INSPIRED ROASTED CARROT AND COCONUT MILK SOUP WITH LIME

• Makes 6 full-sized bowls or 12–16 shooters •

Sweet roasted carrots are added to a rich vegetable soup broth, then enriched by the addition of creamy coconut milk and a medley of aromatics. Once flavored with Thai lime leaf, fresh lemongrass, and spicy chilis, this soup is blended to a silky smoothness, then garnished with cilantro. At a party, it's a perfect appetizer when presented in a small shot glass, but it's so good you might want to serve it by the bowl!

INGREDIENTS

1½ pounds (680 g) whole carrots

1 small (160 g) yellow onion

2 cloves (10 g) garlic, crushed

1 to 2 Thai chilis (can substitute jalapeños for a slightly less spicy soup)

1 tablespoon (15 ml) + 2 teaspoons (10 ml) avocado oil, divided

2 dried Thai lime leaves

32 ounces (900 g) rich vegetable stock, homemade or store bought

6 ounces (180 ml) regular (not "light") coconut milk

2 stalks fresh lemongrass

½ fresh lime, juiced (15 ml juice)

1 cilantro (coriander) bunch (about 80 g)

½ teaspoon (1.5 g) kosher salt + more to taste

INSTRUCTIONS

1. Preheat the oven to 425°F and reserve a large baking tray.

2. Trim the tops off the carrots and peel.

3. Cut the carrots into pieces roughly 2 inches (5 cm) long. Place into a large mixing bowl and add 1 tablespoon (15 ml) of avocado oil and ½ teaspoon (1.5 g) of kosher salt. Mix to coat.

4. Spread the carrots evenly on the large baking tray. Bake for 35–40 minutes, flipping halfway through cooking, then place the tray on a cooling rack.

5. Roughly dice the onion and crush the garlic. Trim and dice the chilis, seeds and all.

6. In a soup pot on medium heat, add 2 teaspoons (10 ml) of avocado oil.

7. Cook the onions and garlic in the oil while stirring occasionally, heating until the onions are slightly translucent but not browned.

8. Once slightly translucent and softened, quickly add the Thai chili(s) and cook for 1 minute.

9. Slice the lemongrass stalks partway through and then "bruise" them by hitting the stalks repeatedly with the back of your knife. This helps release the oils.

10. Add the stock, dried Thai lime leaf, and lemongrass to the soup pot. Shake the coconut milk before opening and add 6 ounces to the pot. Bring to a boil.

11. Add the roasted carrots and reduce the heat to a simmer. Cook for 20 minutes.

12. Remove the pot from the heat; find and discard the lemongrass and dried Thai lime leaf.

13. Working in small batches, blend the soup in a blender until smooth and creamy.

14. Return the soup back to the pot and place over medium heat. Stir in the lime juice and salt to taste.

15. Place a bundle of fresh cilantro into the pot and let it simmer for 5 minutes. Remove the cilantro bundle before serving.

16. Garnish with fried pieces of carrot, a drizzle of coconut milk, and fresh cilantro leaves.

213

SEARED BEEF CROSTINI WITH WASABI MAYONNAISE AND MARINATED CHERRY TOMATOES

This easy appetizer is filled with classic umami flavor and is the perfect bite-sized beef dish. Seared, seasoned steak is sliced thinly, added to toasty pieces of wasabi-mayo-slathered baguette, and topped with a marinated blend of tomatoes and shallot. Each bite is a flavor explosion, and hearty enough to keep your guests satisfied while they celebrate!

INGREDIENTS

For the Marinated Tomatoes

1 cup (150 g) grape tomatoes

2 tablespoons (20 g) shallot, sliced into thin rings

1 tablespoon (15 ml) extra-virgin olive oil

kosher salt

freshly ground black pepper

For the Toasts

1 large French baguette

2 tablespoons (30 ml) extra-virgin olive oil

For the Wasabi Mayonnaise

½ cup (115 g) mayonnaise

1 teaspoon (6.5 g) prepared wasabi

For the Steak

10-ounce (280 g) New York strip (top loin)
or tenderloin steak

kosher salt

freshly ground black pepper

INSTRUCTIONS

For the Marinated Tomatoes

Wash and dry the tomatoes. Slice into thin rings and add to a small mixing bowl. Add the shallots (also cut into rings) to the bowl, along with the red wine vinegar and olive oil. Mix. Season to taste with a pinch of salt and ground black pepper. Reserve.

For the Toasts

1. Set the oven to broil on low and prepare the middle rack. Reserve a large baking tray.

2. Slice a baguette on a bias, into ½-inch-thick (1 cm) portions. Pour out the olive oil into a small bowl and, using a silicone pastry brush or spatula, brush both sides of the bread slices with oil and place on the baking tray.

3. Place the tray into the oven and broil until golden (about 4–5 minutes), flipping halfway. Watch out so you don't burn the bread!

4. Remove from the oven and set on a cooling rack. Reserve.

For the Wasabi Mayonnaise

1. Combine the mayonnaise and wasabi paste in a small bowl, until incorporated.

2. Cover with plastic wrap and chill until use.

For the Steak

1. Season raw steak generously with salt and pepper.

2. Cook to medium rare (or preferred temperature).

3. Rest for 10 minutes and cut into as thin slices as possible.

To Assemble

1. Reserve a large plate or platter.

2. Start by spreading a small amount of the wasabi mayo to each slice of toasted bread.

3. Layer 2–3 thin slices of steak on top and spoon on a layer of the marinated tomatoes.

4. Add to the platter or plate.

5. Garnish with finishing salt and thin rings of scallion.

PORT WINE SABAYON
WITH FRESH BERRIES • Serves 8 •

A sabayon (also known as a zabaglione) is a fantastic dessert sauce, traditionally fortified with sweet wine like Marsala or Riesling. When served on top of a fruit or cake, this custard is sweet, creamy, and deliciously light. This version was created using an aged tawny port in place of the Marsala wine. Even though fresh berries aren't typically a wintertime treat, berries are a grocery store staple and can be found on the shelves any time of year. Easy and elegant, this is a wonderful dessert to serve for a crowd!

INGREDIENTS

3 tablespoons (45 ml) aged tawny port wine

4 large egg yolks

4 tablespoons (60 ml) water

¼ cup (32 g) powdered sugar

½ cup (120 ml) chilled whipping cream (or heavy cream)

3–4 cups (500 g) mixed berries, like raspberries, blueberries, or blackberries

optional garnish:
edible dried flower petals or
edible fresh pansies

INSTRUCTIONS

1. In a medium pot, heat 2–3 inches of water to a simmer (to act as a double boiler). Separately, prepare a large mixing bowl and fill with ice and water, for an ice bath.

2. Place the egg yolks, port wine, water, and sugar into a medium heatproof mixing bowl (when the bowl is fitted over the pot, it should be large enough so that it does not touch the water). Before placing over the heat, whisk the ingredients to combine.

3. Place the bowl over the not-quite-simmering water and whisk continuously for 4 minutes, or until the mixture becomes frothy and thickens.

4. Once thickened, place the bowl with the egg mixture directly into the ice bath. Continue to whisk until the sauce cools, about 3 minutes.

5. With a whisk (or hand mixer) and a medium mixing bowl, whip the chilled cream until it reaches soft peaks (not quite the "firm peak" we associate with whipped cream).

6. Fold the softly whipped cream gently into the cooled egg mixture.

7. Cover the sauce tightly (if using plastic wrap, gently push the plastic into the sauce to prevent a skin form forming). Refrigerate for at least 1 hour (or up to 4 hours).

To Serve

1. Wash and dry your berries. Using small dessert bowls or champagne coupes, portion out the berries evenly.

2. Remove the chilled sabayon from the fridge and give it a quick stir.

3. Spoon on top of the berries and serve immediately.

COCKTAIL PARTY

TABLESCAPE

It's time to ring in the new year with style! I wanted to celebrate this holiday with a lot of classic touches, and elegant flair. Working with a palette of wintry whites, we'll set a table filled with candlelight and flowers, bottles of champagne, and loads of classic cocktail glasses!

COLOR

We'll be primarily using an achromatic/monochromatic color scheme. The bright whites and creams will then be accented with touches of green and gold.

BLOOMS

roses, hydrangea, Queen Anne's lace, lisianthus, willow branches, and various green filler

THE DETAILS

Working with just one color in different shades really amps up the drama but simplifies the decorating process. A stunning floral centerpiece anchors our table, joining several pairs of crystal, wooden, and brass candlesticks. White and colored taper candles bring a warmth to the scene, while trays of vintage cocktail glasses evoke the gilded parties of the past.

WHAT YOU'LL NEED

1 large milk-glass bowl

assorted flowers and greens

neutral-colored table runner

white cloth napkins

gold-toned napkin rings

neutral-colored vintage china dishware

6–8 pairs of candlesticks made of various materials and heights

4 silver glass votive holders with votive candles

marble or white decorative elements such as fruit or shapes

cocktail tray

several sets of glass cocktail glasses, including coupes and Nick and Nora glasses

plenty of champagne!

Set the Table

Location

A large living room, dining room, or hall.

Order of Operations

Place the neutral-colored table runner down the length of the table, with your large, monochromatic floral arrangement in the center, and arrange the silver votive candles around it. Place your candlesticks with candles, in groups of three, around the floral centerpiece. You can also spread out the candlesticks down the length of the table.

Prepare several glasses of champagne and arrange on a cocktail tray. Place fabric napkins with silverware to the side of the table, as well as stacked plates for the hors d'oeuvres.

Small Touches

I've added a separate drink station toward the back of the room, to keep the flow of guests uncrowded. You can serve your hors d'oeuvres on the main table and direct guests toward the back buffet to refill their glass of bubbly. Be sure to add a small floral arrangement and a few candles for a sophisticated touch!

COZY VALENTINE'S DAY DINNER

FRENCH 77 CHAMPAGNE COCKTAIL

A beautifully bubbly three-ingredient champagne cocktail that's sparkling and light. It's sweeter than a glass of bubbly, with a little floral lemon kick.

SMOKED CHEDDAR CHEESE SCALLOPED POTATOES

This dish is decadent and rich! Tender slices of potatoes are layered with a homemade smoked cheddar cheese sauce and baked until bubbling. A wonderful accompaniment to the simple roast chicken. This dish can be made the day before and reheated.

CITRUS AND ROASTED BEET SALAD WITH HONEYED VINAIGRETTE

Sweet citrus and delicately sweet roasted beets make a sweet and tart counterpoint to cut the richness of the cheesy potatoes on this menu. Garnished with fresh basil leaves and topped with a light honey champagne vinegar dressing. The vinaigrette and the beets can be made the day before, if desired. See page 29.

WHOLE ROASTED CHICKEN WITH FRESH THYME

A stunning main course that couldn't be easier! Flavorful juicy chicken meat and crispy skin, flavored with salt, pepper, and fresh thyme. A simple and elegant whole bird for two.

PECAN PRALINE CHEESECAKE WITH BOURBON CARAMEL SAUCE

An impressive dessert that is sure to steal your sweetie's heart! Flavored with bourbon and vanilla, this cheesecake is topped with a sinfully good bourbon caramel sauce and brown-sugar-candied pecans. This dish can be prepared the day before the event, but keep the components separate until just before serving.

FRENCH 77 CHAMPAGNE COCKTAIL

• Makes two 5-ounce cocktails •

Effervescent and delicately sweet, this elegant combination of elderflower liqueur and champagne is delicious. With only three ingredients, and topped with a pretty floral garnish, this champagne cocktail couldn't be easier.

INGREDIENTS

2 ounces (60 ml) elderflower liqueur

1 teaspoon (15 ml) fresh lemon juice

8 ounces (240 ml) semisweet
(demi-sec) champagne

fresh lemon peel (without pith)

ice

for garnish: edible fresh flowers such
as pansies or violets

INSTRUCTIONS

1. Chill two champagne flutes or wine glasses in the freezer.

2. Cut or shave several thin slivers of peel and reserve (being careful not to include the bitter white pith). Juice the lemon and reserve.

3. Pour the elderflower liqueur and lemon juice into the cup of a cocktail strainer. Add a handful of ice. Close and quickly shake to chill.

4. Using the prechilled glasses, divide the chilled lemon elderflower mixture evenly into each glass.

5. Top each glass with 4 ounces (120 ml) of chilled champagne.

6. Garnish with lemon peel and edible flowers.

SMOKED CHEDDAR CHEESE SCALLOPED POTATOES

• Serves 8–10 •

A cozy comfort-food classic. This rich, comforting, and indulgent dish is a delicious side for your Valentine's Day dinner. Thinly sliced Yukon Gold potatoes are layered with a homemade cheese sauce, made using smoked cheddar and Monterey Jack. Baked until bubbling, this is a potato recipe to fall in love with!

INGREDIENTS

2 pounds (900 g) Yukon Gold potatoes

¼ cup (56 g) butter

4 small (240 g) shallots, minced

1 clove (5 g) fresh garlic, minced

¼ cup (32 g) all-purpose flour

2½ cups (600 ml) whole milk

1 cup (110 g) shredded smoked cheddar cheese

½ cup (60 g) shredded Monterey Jack cheese

kosher salt

freshly ground black pepper

INSTRUCTIONS

1. Preheat the oven to 350°F and reserve a 3-quart (13-by-9-inch, or 23 × 33 cm) casserole dish for baking.

2. Wash and peel the potatoes. Using a mandoline slicer, slice the potatoes into ⅛-inch-thick (0.25 cm) rounds. You can also do this step by hand with a sharp knife.

3. Place the potato slices into a large mixing bowl of ice water to prevent browning.

4. Mince the garlic and shallots.

5. In a Dutch oven or large skillet, melt the butter over medium heat, until foamy.

6. Add the garlic and shallots to the melted butter and cook until slightly translucent and soft. Stir occasionally. Lower the temperature if the aromatics start to brown. About 5 minutes.

7. Add the flour, a pinch of salt, and several grinds of fresh black pepper to the pot.

8. Continue stirring and add the flour into the pot with the aromatics, cooking the mix until it reaches a light-brown color and has a "nutty" smell. This takes about 3 minutes. This is the roux for the cheese sauce.

9. Next, add the milk to the pot and continue stirring. It will become incorporated into the roux. Although the milk will initially seem very liquidy, it will suddenly seem to be "soaked up" into the roux and become thicker. Heat until the sauce reaches a low simmer and has thickened to coat the back of a spoon, about 5–7 minutes.

10. After thickening, remove the pot from the heat and add half of the shredded cheese to the sauce base. Stir to combine. Adjust the salt and pepper to taste.

11. Drain the potatoes in a colander over the sink and return to the mixing bowl.

12. Take the casserole dish and spread a thin layer of the cheese sauce over the bottom.

13. Next, start to layer your potato slices in a shingle pattern (overlapping rows) in one layer over the bottom of the pan. The potatoes should resemble fish scales when layered correctly. Spread a pinch of salt over the potatoes to season them.

14. Add half of the cheese sauce over the first layer of potatoes. Sprinkle the remaining shredded cheese on top.

15. Repeat another overlapping layer of potato slices and spread the last of the cheese sauce on top.

16. Cover the casserole dish tightly with aluminum foil and bake on the center rack of the oven for 40 minutes at 350°F.

17. After 40 minutes, uncover the casserole dish and continue to bake for 25–30 minutes, until bubbling and slightly golden on top.

18. Remove from the oven and place on a cooling rack. Let stand for 15 minutes before serving.

WHOLE ROASTED CHICKEN
WITH FRESH THYME   • Makes 1 whole chicken; serves 4 •

If there is any dish worth presenting to the love of your life, it must be a straight-from-the-oven whole roast chicken. This bird is simply trussed, then seasoned with salt, black pepper, and fresh thyme leaves. It's even more simple to roast—it's popped into a very hot oven and left alone. I'll show you how to do a simple truss, step by step, so you can impress with this easy, juicy roasted chicken.

INGREDIENTS

1 whole chicken, weighing about 3 pounds (1,400 g)

kosher salt

ground black pepper

6 sprigs fresh thyme

butcher's twine

INSTRUCTIONS

To Prepare the Chicken

1. Preheat the oven to 400°F (convection) or 425°F (regular bake).

2. Remove the chicken from the wrapping (if any) and rinse it briefly in the sink. Pat dry with paper towels. Make sure there are no giblets inside the bird. If the neck is present, it can be trimmed off as well.

3. To keep the chicken out of the pan juices, the wings will be tucked under the body to prop it up—this will keep the good bits out of the juices that will collect in the pan/skillet.

4. To tuck the wings, twist them 180° around, toward the back of the chicken, and tuck them under the body. You will have to loosen the connective tissue to do this, but in the end the chicken should look propped up on "elbows" on the nonbreast side. This will keep the chicken elevated.

5. Using kosher salt, generously salt the inside and outside of the carcass. This helps flavor the meat directly, but it will draw out any extra water for a more intense flavor.

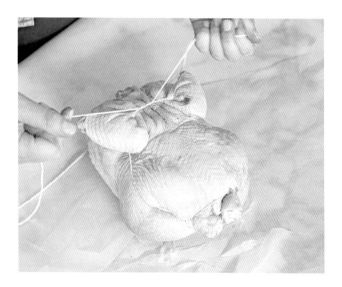

How to Truss

There are many ways to truss a bird, but I have found that this simple way works beautifully:

1. Take a long piece of butcher's twine and place under the ends of the drumsticks, crossing the twine over to pull the legs together tightly.

2. Now tuck the twine around the wings and then turn the bird over, cinching tightly again by tying a knot in the midline. Trim the excess string. You're done!

3. The legs should look like they are hugging the side of the bird, which makes the chicken cook more evenly by pulling the drumsticks in toward the body, forming one large single mass.

Season and Roast

1. Sprinkle freshly ground pepper and thyme leaves over the top and sides of the chicken.

2. Place the chicken in an oven-safe pan and into the pre-heated oven.

3. Cook for about 45 minutes at 400°F (for a 3-pound bird) on convection cook. If using *normal baking mode*, raise the temperature to *425°F*. The chicken will be ready to remove when it reaches about 150°F internally (it will continue cooking to approximately 165°F when you remove it from the oven, due to the residual heat—the outside is hotter than the core, and that extra heat will continue to transfer).

4. Rest for 5–10 minutes to finish the cooking before removing the twine.

5. Discard the butcher's twine and serve!

PECAN PRALINE CHEESECAKE
WITH BOURBON CARAMEL SAUCE · Serves 10–12 ·

This luxurious cheesecake can't help but receive loads of "wow" from the table! It's baked on top of a classic graham cracker crumb crust, coated with a rich bourbon caramel sauce, then topped with cinnamon and brown-sugar-candied pecans.

INGREDIENTS

For the Crust

2 cups (240 g) crushed graham crackers
(about 2 packages of 8 crackers)

6 tablespoons (85 g) melted butter

2 tablespoons (25 g) sugar

¼ teaspoon (0.6 g) ground cinnamon

1 pinch (1.2 g) kosher salt

For the Cheesecake Batter

32 ounces (908 g), or 4 blocks, of cream cheese,
at room temperature

1½ cups (300 g) sugar

4 eggs (220 g total)

1 tablespoon (15 ml) bourbon, optional

1½ teaspoon (7 g) vanilla extract

½ teaspoon (1.5 g) kosher salt

special equipment:

1 9-inch (23 cm) springform pan

1 sheet of parchment paper, cut into a circle
to fit the springform pan

4 large sheets of aluminum foil

1 large cast-iron pan (12 inch / 30 cm) or
other large oven-safe shallow vessel

INSTRUCTIONS

For the Crust

1. Preheat the oven to 350°F and prepare the middle rack for baking.

2. Line the springform pan with a round of parchment.

3. Take the graham crackers and crush in a food processor (or by hand), until you have fine crumbs. Place into a large mixing bowl.

4. Melt the 6 tablespoons of butter, either on the stovetop or in a nonmetallic bowl in the microwave.

5. Pour the melted butter onto the graham cracker crumbs. Add the sugar, salt, and ground cinnamon to the crumbs as well, then use a fork to mix until the crumbs are moistened.

6. Transfer the crumb mixture to the springform pan and press evenly to create the crust. Push the mixture up the sides (at least halfway) and press down firmly to create a nice even crust.

7. Bake in the oven for 10–12 minutes (as a blind bake), until lightly browned. Remove from the oven and allow to cool to room temperature on a baking rack until use.

For the Cheesecake Batter

1. Begin by lowering the oven temperature to 325°F.

2. In a kettle, boil 4 cups (about 1 L) of water. We will be using a water bath to bake the cheesecake more evenly.

3. Using a stand mixer with paddle attachment (or a hand mixer and a large bowl), beat the softened cream cheese on medium-high speed, until creamed (about 3–5 minutes). Scrape down the sides of the bowl if needed.

4. Add the sugar and continue to beat for one minute.

5. On low-medium speed, add in each egg individually and beat until incorporated. Wait to add the next egg until the previous one has been evenly mixed into the batter. Scrape down the sides so you don't get lumps of plain cream cheese, but be careful not to overbeat—this can add too much air to the cake batter and cause it to fall (crater) in the oven.

6. On low-medium speed, add the bourbon (optional), vanilla extract, and salt. Beat until combined. About 1 minute.

Preparing the Pan for the Water Bath

1. Taking 4 large sheets of foil, the goal is to construct an easy protective liner for the cheesecake as it bakes in the water bath. Using 2 sheets of foil, fold the horizontal edges together to make 1 large sheet. Crunch the seam to make it "seal." Do the same with the next 2 sheets.

2. Now that the 4 sheets of foil have been made into 2 larger sheets, place them on top of each other; one seam should be horizontal and one vertical. We are trying to prevent any of the water bath from leaking into the cake.

3. Place the springform pan into the middle of the foil, then scrunch and fold around the pan. Keep the top of the foil from touching the top lip of the pan.

4. "Nest" the springform pan into your larger baking vessel (such as a large cast-iron skillet). Make sure there is room around the pan for the boiling water. This two-pan setup is essentially a protective layer of water around your cheesecake to make sure it absorbs heat more evenly and slowly.

To Bake

1. Pour the cheesecake filling onto the prepared crust in the springform pan, then lightly smooth the top out with a rubber spatula or small offset palette knife.

2. Very carefully, pour the boiling water into the larger cooking vessel, so that it surrounds the "waterproofed" foil-wrapped springform pan. Pour the water halfway up the sides of the pan. Be mindful not to spill any water into the cheesecake batter.

3. After preparing the water bath, gently (while wearing oven gloves) transfer the whole vessel (without spilling the water bath surrounding the cheesecake) into the oven and bake on the middle rack for 1 hour and 15 minutes, or until set. Rotate the cheesecake around halfway through baking. The center should be just set when done.

4. After baking, set two wire cooling racks on your counter. Place a dish towel under one of them to catch any spilling water. Remove the entire vessel to one cooling rack.

5. Remove the cheesecake to stop it from cooking in the water bath, by very gently lifting the foil-wrapped springform pan and placing it on the other cooling rack.

6. While wearing oven gloves, or using utensils, carefully peel the foil away to allow the springform to cool faster.

7. Move the larger vessel to the side and allow the cheesecake, in the springform, to cool to room temperature.

8. Cover and refrigerate. Chill the cheesecake for at least 6 hours (or overnight) before serving.

9. To remove from the springform, gently run a sharp knife around the edge of the cheesecake and then unsnap the springform pan. The parchment paper we placed at the bottom of the cake will let you transfer the cake to a plate easily.

To Serve

Top with caramel sauce and candied pecans. A dollop of freshly whipped cream is a nice touch too!

Homemade Bourbon Caramel Sauce

Completely addictive, yet simple to make, this rich caramel sauce is delicious on cheesecake, as well as ice cream and tarts.

• Makes about 2½ cups (600 ml) •

INGREDIENTS

2 cups (400 g) sugar

¾ cup (180 ml) heavy cream

1½ teaspoon (7 g) vanilla extract

1 tablespoon (15 ml) bourbon, optional

1 pinch (1.2 g) kosher salt

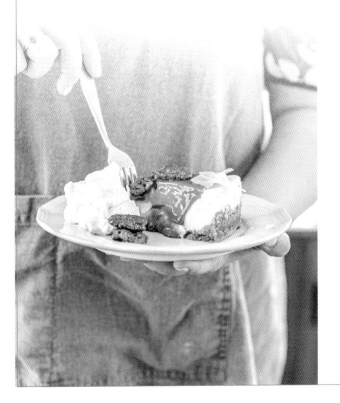

INSTRUCTIONS

1. Due to the importance of timing when working with sugar at high temperatures, be sure to have all your ingredients pre-portioned and all your tools ready to use.

2. Place a large saucepan over medium-high heat. Add the sugar and let melt. Stir occasionally, with a goal of melting the sugar low and slow. The large saucepan provides a greater surface area for heat distribution.

3. Continue to stir until the sugar becomes a liquid. Be very careful not to burn the sugar, and lower the heat if the sugar starts to scorch. Cook for about 10 minutes.

4. After the sugar has melted into a brown, viscous liquid, lower the heat and put on your oven mitts to protect your hands.

5. Carefully add the heavy cream into the sugar and, using a whisk, stir down the bubbles. This will cause a dramatic boiling-like reaction! It's important that you wear protective mitts during this step!

6. Continue to whisk the sugar and cream until it becomes a thickened sauce, which should take about 3 minutes. The caramel will be a rich-brown color, and syrupy.

7. Remove the pot from the heat and whisk in the vanilla extract, salt, and bourbon (if desired).

8. Let cool slightly, then pour into a large glass jar with a lid. Close and let cool to room temperature.

9. Chill to store until use. Before using, if desired, the jar can be placed in a pot of water, slowly bringing the water around the jar to a simmer to reheat (this also works to uncrystallize honey!)

Cinnamon Brown-Sugar-Candied Pecans

Crunchy, sweet, and nutty, these pecans are lovely in desserts and as a salad topping.

• Makes 1½ cups (180 g) •

INGREDIENTS

1½ cups (170 g) raw whole pecans

¾ cup (90 g) light brown sugar

2 tablespoons (30 ml) water

1 teaspoon (2.5 g) ground cinnamon

¼ teaspoon (0.7 g) ground ginger

1 pinch (1.2 g) kosher salt

INSTRUCTIONS

1. Preheat the oven to 350°F and line the baking sheet with parchment paper.

2. Spread the raw pecans on the baking sheet and roast for about 5–7 minutes, or until fragrant. Check frequently, since nuts can burn easily.

3. Remove the oven and place on a wire rack to cool.

4. Place a large skillet on medium-high heat and add the brown sugar, water, salt, and spices. Mix well.

5. Stir and cook until the sugar melts.

6. Add the toasted pecans to the melted sugar mixture and stir to coat (keep the baking sheet and paper ready).

7. Let cook for about 5 minutes, while stirring. Lower the heat if you notice the nuts are browning too quickly. The candy coating will become slightly shiny when done and should not be sticky at the end.

8. Spread the candied nuts in one layer on the parchment paper. Let cool to room temperature.

9. Store in an airtight container until use.

COZY

VALENTINE'S DAY DINNER

TABLESCAPE

Valentine's Day is definitely the right time to pull out all the romantic stops when it comes to setting the table! For my love-filled table, roses and candlelight are a classic match, but I've added even more warmth and whimsical details to make your night even more special.

COLOR

Our Valentine's Day flower story features just one mesmerizing color: a gorgeous red. Though the flowers are monochromatic, when we add the amber votives and glasses, the whole table acts as an analogous color scheme.

BLOOMS

'Black Magic' roses

THE DETAILS

Romance is in the air! By using just one type and color of velvety rose, we've not only simplified our centerpiece's arrangement but added a seductive and dramatic element to the table. The pop of yellow from the glassware, combined with the neutral-colored dishware, creates a message of "exciting and inviting."

WHAT YOU'LL NEED

1 low square vase or 2 low cylinder glass vases

24 'Black Magic' roses

1 ivory-colored table runner

white cotton napkins with embroidered detailing

ivory or neutral-colored dishware, with textural details

crystal champagne flutes

amber-colored goblets

amber-colored glass votives

silver-colored glass votives

white votive candles

2 small glass bottles

2 small pieces of paper

twine

dried flowers

paper heart confetti

Set the Table

Location

A large dining room or living room.

Order of Operations

Place the neutral-colored table runner across the length of the table. Add the one large (or use two smaller) rose arrangement to the center of the table. Sprinkle some paper heart confetti around the rose centerpiece. Place the amber and silver glass votives staggered around the centerpiece. Arrange your table settings with one dinner plate, one salad plate, and one napkin folded into a rectangle. Set your decorative "love note" (see below) in a bottle on top of the napkin. Lay your silverware and place your amber drinking goblets on the table. Set the crystal champagne flutes off to the side of each setting.

Small Touches

I've assembled small love notes as a placeholder for this table scene. Simply insert your favorite love poem or quote, printed on a piece of small craft paper, into the little glass bottle. Decorate with dried flowers and tie with twine.

ACKNOWLEDGMENTS

This book owes its existence to so many kind and talented people from all areas of my world. It might have stayed confined to a few scribbled pages in an old spiral-bound notebook, without the help and support of too many people to mention. But I will try my best and beg forgiveness for those not included!

I want to say a truly heartfelt thank-you the readers and fans of *Straight to the Hips, Baby*. You've been by my side through all the highs and lows over the last four years. Your enthusiasm to try new recipes and your gracious comments, family stories, and support mean the world to me.

A huge thank-you must go to my husband, Jonathan Ross. He is my head photographer, chief taste tester, and diligent recipe metric converter. Without you, Jon, this book would not be. It has been such a joyful, sometimes exasperating, and most definitely giggle-inducing pleasure to work side by side! I couldn't imagine this amazing life without you. I love you, my sweet Canuck.

A tremendous thank-you to my editor, Sandra Korinchak, who was always positive and patient with my text (sorry about all the commas!) and my vision. Writing a book detailing my passion for home entertaining, flowers, and food has always been a dream, and Sandra was there every step of the way.

Thank you to Danielle Farmer, Hannah Brown, and everyone on the amazing team at Schiffer Publishing for taking a chance on my concept and diving headfirst into this adventure. I am so grateful for your dedicated hard work on this genre-blending book, which I hope will not only entertain but inspire home cooks and floral-loving hosts across the world.

Thank you to Monica Michelle, for giving me one of my first "big breaks" and so many opportunities to share my passion for food, flowers, and home entertaining. The world needs more "connectors" and innovators like you.

A grateful thank-you must be said to the food creators, educators, colleagues, and flower folk who are my dear friends, both online and in person. Thank you to Shelly Waldman, Nicole Leverett, Alyson Brown, and the entire Food Blog School hub; you are my community and continuously inspire me to dream bigger and reach higher. To my flower friends Jamie Jamison, Dionne Woods, Lori Siebert, Katie Lila, Jennifer Gulizia, and Ashley Rodriguez: meeting and collaborating with you was a huge turning point for me, and I am incredibly grateful for your wisdom.

Thank you to the hosts, producers, and crews at the television stations that I have been so fortunate to film with over the last several years. Your talents and kindness have paved the way for me not only to bring *Straight to the Hips, Baby* to a wider audience, but to help give me the confidence to take that leap forward into the bigger entertainment world.

Alexander, Benjamin, and Harrison: thank you, my sweet little boys. You patiently lived on PB&J sandwiches and test batches of over-the-top desserts for six months, never ever complaining. You helped inspire recipes, taste-test, and hold light diffusers to get that perfect shot. I love each of you, infinity plus one.

A huge thank-you to my family, and friends who are family. My brother Lucas Roman, and the Ross, the Jacobs, and the Fleming clans: you have been my guinea pigs, sounding boards, advisors, and enthusiastic cheering section. Cotton Wright, Jamie Brown, and Erika Wolf: You kept me giggling, lent support from afar, and made sure that I drank my water every day. We might have met in the ballet studio all those years ago, but we are family for life.

Thank you to my Western Mass village for lending me your positivity and embracing my family here in the mountains. Thank you also to the holiday host with the most, Angela Egan, for acting as my festive season prop house. Special thanks to Jaimie and Joe Cambi for letting me set gorgeous scenes in their fairy-tale backyard. Thank you to Tara and Derek Rosner for allowing me to crash your magazine-worthy kitchen to capture the perfect cover shot. Your homes and gardens lent such a special touch to my table scenes and managed to pull me out of my own kitchen during the long days of writing as well!

Last, thank you to those dear family who are no longer with us but planted the seeds of this book by example and memory. With each new season and beautiful holiday table, I remember you.

VEGAN AND GLUTEN-FREE CHANGES FOR SELECTED RECIPES

So many of my friends and family follow specific dietary requirements, both by choice or by need. I count myself in that group as well, with gluten sensitivity that makes me pause before enjoying any regular old plate of pasta! It's important as a host to cater to your guests' needs with recipes that are not only absolutely delicious, but also suitable for many different preferences.

I've selected several recipes from each seasonal menu in this book and adjusted the ingredients to reflect either convenient vegan choices or gluten-free changes. I recommend speaking to your guests ahead of time as a general practice, to find out if there are any dietary preferences or allergies before you set your menu. It's a thoughtful act and it's always appreciated!

SPRING

Creamy Basil Dip with Fresh Vegetables, page 28

Vegan: Replace the dairy Greek yogurt with plain unsweetened almond milk yogurt. Swap the honey in the dip for agave nectar.

Citrus and Roasted Beet Salad with Honeyed Vinaigrette, page 29

Vegan: Substitute agave nectar for the honey in the vinaigrette.

Mozzarella Pesto Toasts with Crispy Pancetta and Pickled Rhubarb, page 42

GF: Use gluten-free sourdough bread.

Mini Sugar Cookie Lemon Tarts, page 59

GF: Replace the all-purpose flour with *Bob's Red Mill Gluten Free 1-to-1 Baking Flour*. This is one of my favorite products to bake gluten-free cookies and brownies.

Savory Turkey Meatballs with Roasted Balsamic Tomatoes and
Celery Root Puree, page 71

GF: Replace the panko breadcrumbs with your favorite gluten-free version, as well as using a gluten-free balsamic vinegar for the roasted tomato sauce.

Sweet Nectarine Cake with Whipped Vanilla Buttercream Frosting, page 73

GF: Replace the all-purpose flour with *Bob's Red Mill Gluten Free 1-to-1 Baking Flour*.

SUMMER

Baked Mac and Cheese with Crispy Cornflake Topping, page 85

GF: Swap out the regular pasta for your favorite gluten-free spiral pasta. Replace the all-purpose flour in the roux with 4 tablespoons (32 g) of ground arrowroot powder. You can leave out the traditional cornflake cereal topping or utilize an organic gluten-free version found in your local natural-foods store.

My Favorite Hamburger, page 97

Vegan: Substitute an equal portion of *Impossible Plant Based Beef Ground* for the ground beef listed. Leave the egg out entirely and replace the Worcestershire sauce with 2 teaspoons (11 g) of organic aged Japanese soy sauce. The distinct umami flavor from the soy sauce will play nicely with the spices.

AUTUMN

Vanilla Chai Pear Bundt Cake, page 143

GF: Replace the all-purpose flour with *Bob's Red Mill Gluten Free 1-to-1 Baking Flour*.

Crispy Smashed Baby Potatoes with Garlic, Herbs, and Feta Cheese, page 167

Vegan: Leave the feta cheese to the side and substitute dairy-free and vegan feta crumbles.

Apple and Pear Crumble, page 178

GF/Vegan: Replace the dairy butter with equal amounts of vegan European-style plant-based butter. To make this recipe gluten-free as well, swap the all-purpose flour for *Bob's Red Mill Gluten Free 1-to-1 Baking Flour.*

WINTER

Classic Potato Latkes with Sweet and Savory Garnishes, page 188

Vegan: Replace the traditional dairy sour cream with your favorite almond milk or cashew milk plant-based sour cream. This recipe is already gluten-free and makes a great appetizer during the colder months!

Dark Chocolate and Tahini Brownies with Gelt, page 193

GF: Replace the all-purpose flour with *Bob's Red Mill Gluten Free 1-to-1 Baking Flour* and be sure to use a gluten-free brand of sesame tahini.

Peppermint White Hot Chocolate, page 199

GF/Vegan: Replace the dairy milk with your favorite plant-based milk (I prefer a coconut/cashew milk blend). Choose a gluten-free vegan white-chocolate-chip brand and follow the directions as written. I love some of the ready-made coconut whip in the grocery store as a topping, and it's convenient too.

Jessie-Sierra Ross is a food and lifestyle blogger and television food personality and is the imagination behind the blog *Straight to the Hips, Baby*. A former professional ballerina from Boston, Jessie traded in her fast-paced urban life for the farm-to-table landscape of Western Massachusetts. She is known for her easy elegance and floral-touched style of cooking, cocktails, and home entertaining. With an emphasis on scratch cooking and a hands-on approach to party planning, Jessie-Sierra reaches national audiences as a regular creator and contributor on BloomTV Network, PBS, CBS, and New England–area NBC morning shows. Jessie-Sierra has helped educate and build the confidence of countless home cooks and budding hosts for over a decade.

straighttothehipsbaby.com

Instagram: @straighttothehipsbaby

Facebook: straighttothehipsbaby

Pinterest: @STTHbaby

TikTok: @STTHBaby